The Bailiff's Son

The Bailiff's Son

THE LIFE OF
JACK SEARS

As told to
Brenda Frith

ISIS
LARGE PRINT
Oxford

First published in Great Britain 2006
by Isis Publishing Ltd.

Published in Large Print 2006 by ISIS Publishing Ltd.,
7 Centremead, Osney Mead, Oxford OX2 0ES
by arrangement with the author

British Library Cataloguing in Publication Data
Frith, Brenda
      The bailiff's son : the life of Jack Sears.
      – Large print ed.
      (Isis reminiscence series)
      1. Sears, Jack
      2. Gardeners – Great Britain – Biography
      3. Large type books
      I. Title
      635'.092

ISBN 0–7531–9350–7 (hb)
ISBN 0–7531–9351–5 (pb)

Printed and bound in Great Britain by
T. J. International Ltd., Padstow, Cornwall

Preface

I met Jack Sears when I moved into a house called Chivers Lodge and found he was my nearest neighbour. He told me he had once lived in Chivers Lodge himself and I asked him how this came about. He explained the reason and then, gradually, came to tell me more and more about his life. How he had spent his childhood and most of his adult years living and working on private country estates. Aware that he was talking of a way of life which has gone forever I decided his recollections about this and other events he had experienced were worth recording in written form.

Brenda Frith

CHAPTER
ONE

I was born in a rural corner of Hertfordshire. The day was the thirteenth, the month August, the year 1893. Victoria was Queen, Gladstone, Prime Minister. Recently I went back to the place where I entered the world and spent my early life. Today, busy wide roads slice through it, but I could still walk along the narrow lanes I knew as a child. And recognize many of the fields and patches of woodland where I played as a boy. The landscape has not changed so very much over the years, though the people have. Those living there now have a totally different way of life from the one I remember. When I was a boy, most were ordinary country folk like my own family. And many of them depended on the local private country estates for their living, just as my father did.

At the time I was born, a chain of private country estates crisscrossed most of the surrounding Hertfordshire countryside. They took in endless cultivated fields, vast stretches of woodland, numerous dairy farms and dozens of tiny cottages. As well as employment, these estates could offer an ordinary young country boy a cottage as a home for any family he might have later. My father had been just such an ordinary country boy.

I have always answered to the name Jack, although I was christened John after my father, John Sears. When I was born, he was working on a small private country estate called Colney Park, 200 flat fertile acres sited at the junction of two roads. The one on the estate's eastern boundary joined London Colney, our nearest village, to Shenley, a neighbouring one. The other skirted its southern border and linked Colney Heath, another small village, to the village of Radlett.

At that time, the horse was still undisputed "King of the Road" (although for faster travel, over longer distances, people turned to the "iron horse", the railway) so London Colney had a resident blacksmith, wheelwright and saddler. *Kelly's Directory* listed London Colney as being "three and a half miles east of Radlett station on the Midland railway, five north-west from Potters Bar station on the Great Northern railway, three south-east from St Albans, six north-west from Barnet and seventeen from London". A Mr Kingham owned the Colney Park estate. A "gentleman" farmer, he delegated total responsibility for its day-to-day running to his Bailiff. My father had worked hard all his life and his hard work helped him climb the private country estate employment ladder. He held the top job of Bailiff on the estate.

My father spent his working day organising all the outdoor workers employed on the estate. He had to ensure that crops, such as wheat and barley, were planted, weeded and harvested. He also supervised three gardeners, one of them senior to the other two. They took care of the flowerbeds, or "pleasure gardens" as they were known, around the "big house", tended the fruit and vegetables in the large kitchen garden and kept the orchard behind it in good order. In addition, my father kept a careful eye on two gamekeepers. Mr Kingham liked to invite his friends for a weekend of rough shooting. As was usual in those days, I lived on the estate where my father worked. My father, my mother, my sister Alice Elizabeth, two years older than myself, and my brother Stanley, three years younger, were the family I knew as a boy. Eventually I had another brother, but William arrived some 15 years after I was born.

Because my father was the Bailiff, our family cottage, Colney Park Lodge, was bigger than those given to the ordinary workers on the estate. And, unlike theirs, it was not one of a pair. A section of the high wall surrounding the kitchen garden formed one side of it. A thick layer of shiny green ivy clung to the other three. Our cottage did not stand next to the main gate as its name suggests. It was quite near the "big house", not far from two other estate workers' homes, but a small copse of tall trees screened the three of them. All the workers on the estate and their families used the side gate on the Shenley Road. Only the residents of the "big house" and their guests entered or left the estate through the main gates.

Our front door opened on to a large hall. The dining room was on the right. We ate our evening meal in there on weekdays and all our main meals at the weekend, sitting at a large round mahogany table with a centre leg. A large oval mirror hung above the open fireplace.

A selection of family photographs decorated the remaining three walls. More were displayed on our upright piano. A settee and two big armchairs occupied the drawing room opposite. Sometimes, my mother played the organ in there on Sunday, hymn tunes only. Again, family photographs hung on each wall.

Further along the hall, a small door concealed a tiny cellar under the stairs. My father kept his tin of tobacco and a half-gallon keg of beer in there. The kitchen was at the back of the house behind the dining room. It housed our enormous black cooking range which consisted of a very large oven with a space for a fire next to it. When we wanted to boil water in our kettle or cook food in our saucepans, we stood them on an iron trivet fixed over the fire. We never worried about the amount of coal we heaped on our kitchen fire or those in our dining and drawing rooms. A generous free supply was part of my father's wages.

My father used to light the kitchen fire most mornings. But as we children got older, occasionally we would light it instead. However, no-one had to wait until the kitchen fire was roaring away before they could have a hot cup of tea. We used to boil our kettle on a small "Beatrix" paraffin stove. If the weather were cold, we lit both its two burners. Together, they gave out quite a good heat, so we soon had the comfort of a warm kitchen as well as a hot drink. A small scullery was opposite the kitchen. It had a large brown earthenware sink, but the outlet pipe did not feed into a proper drain. Instead it went into a simple soakaway under the scullery window.

Upstairs were four bedrooms. Only the "big houses" had bathrooms. My mother and father slept in one bedroom, Alice in another and Stanley and I in the third. The fourth was kept for visitors. Poor Aunt Mary-Ann used it regularly. She was a pleasant enough old dear and generous, too. She slipped me many a shiny silver sixpence, and she gave them to Alice and Stanley, as well. But none of us could really take to her. We were put off by the pungent odour of wintergreen ointment, her favourite cure for her rheumatism.

Our beds had iron bedsteads and plump feather mattresses. But the mattresses got flattened as we slept, so they had to be vigorously shaken and "turned" every day. Then they were ready, soft and comfortable, for the next night. We did not have a piped water supply. None of the workers' cottages did. So I had a large jug and bowl in my bedroom. The jug stood inside the bowl on a marble-topped washstand. The idea was this. At night I filled my jug with water. Then next morning, I tipped the water into the bowl so I could have a wash. But, to be truthful, my morning wash tended to be rather a token procedure, especially in winter. I have often had to stand shivering while I broke through a layer of ice before I could pour out the water underneath. Sometimes I found it was impossible. The water was simply one solid frozen mass. Many an icy morning I have seen my father ram the poker in the kitchen fire and leave it there until it was glowing red-hot. Then he would race upstairs and plunge it into one of the jugs, melting the ice and, hopefully, making the water underneath a shade less chilly.

My father never shaved in the morning, whatever the weather or season. Neither did the other workers. The men usually shaved and washed themselves thoroughly at the end of the day, before sitting down to their evening meal. By that time, all the fires were alight and sufficient hot water was available.

I did have a regular bath night. It was Friday. We used to haul our old tin bath out of the scullery and dump it on the floor in front of the kitchen fire. Then we filled it with all the hot water we had managed to boil in our kettle and saucepans. As we had such a limited supply, we three children made do with one bathful between us. Because she was a girl, Alice went first into the clean water. I went in second. Stanley was last. My mother, meanwhile, kept topping up the bath with an extra saucepan or two of hot water. Afterwards, we children were sent to bed while our parents had their baths.

The large white jug and bowl in my bedroom were sprinkled with a pretty pattern of small pink and red flowers. A matching pattern decorated the large white chamber pot tucked under my bed. Shops usually sold these items in matching sets of three. Like everyone else, I considered the chamber pot, or "goes under" as it was known locally, the most important item in my bedroom. Apart from the bed, of course.

The reason stood a few steps from our backdoor: a small brick building about the size of a sentry box, partially screened by a low brick wall. It housed the family's outdoor toilet. We took it for granted. All the estate workers' cottages were similarly equipped. But no-one fancied creeping out to them in the middle of the night. Especially if it were freezing cold, or there was blizzarding snow or drenching rain. That was when the "goes under" came in handy.

Our outdoor toilet was a simple earth closet, a plank of wood fixed from wall to wall at knee height, with a circular hole cut in the middle. Underneath the hole a pit was dug in the earth floor. Of course, in time, the pit had to be emptied. But we were lucky. Because my father was the Bailiff we did not have to do the job ourselves. The other workers on the estate emptied it for us. I believe the men took it in turns to do the job and I think my father handed over a small sum of money afterwards, as a personal thank you. Two of them used to come at night, after dark. I do not know whether this was to spare us any embarrassment, or whether they did not have time to do it during the day. But we children always knew what was going on. You could never mistake the smell.

The men used to bring with them a length of rope, two buckets and a large wooden barrel. Using the rope, they would lower the buckets, in turn, into the pit and empty them into the barrel. Then each time the barrel was full, they carried it round to the orchard and spread the contents over the roots of the fruit trees. It was reckoned to be the best fertiliser of all.

Because we had no piped water supply we used to collect rainwater from the roof in a large metal water butt standing just to the left of our front door. The water butt had a wooden lid to cover the top and a tap at the bottom. Apart from the rainwater in the water butt, every drop we needed had to be carried to our cottage from a well nearby. But again, we were lucky. Because my father was the Bailiff, the two under-gardeners used to go to the well to get water for us. Our kitchen window opened onto the kitchen garden and my mother would call to them whenever the buckets holding our supply were empty. Usually one of them was working within earshot either there or in the orchard behind it. But if both happened to be working in a place which was too far away for them to hear her, a short ring on her little hand bell soon attracted their attention.

Drawing water from the well was hard work, especially on washdays and bath nights. I know because when I was older I helped to do it. There were no mechanical means of winching your bucket up and down. A low brick wall circled the top of the well. It had an iron bar fixed across it. A length of rope was attached to the iron bar and a large hook was fixed to the other end of the rope. I put the handle of my bucket over the hook. Then I eased the rope slowly through my fingers. I had to lower my bucket very gently down into the water at the bottom of the well or I risked losing my bucket. When the bucket was full, I hauled it back up again. Even more slowly now, because the bucket was very heavy indeed.

When we three children were very young, my mother constantly worried about the attraction the well and its water might have for us. So we were forbidden to go anywhere near it. But one day Stanley and I decided deliberately to flout this rule. I think the well attracted

8

us all the more precisely because it was forbidden territory. There we stood, playfully swinging the end of the rope from one to the other across the top of the well. Suddenly, one time when it was Stanley's turn to catch it, he leaned forward with his hand out but somehow his hand missed the rope. The iron hook on the end hit him in the face, slashing his cheek open. He had the scar for the rest of his life. My father gave both of us a good hiding when he came home. After that, we did not dare go near the well for a very long time.

CHAPTER
TWO

A small stream, the beginning of the River Colne, ran through the Colney Park estate. This may have provided the Colney part of its name. At one point, just a field away from our cottage, a tiny man-made island perched in the middle of it. Everyone called it Chantry Island. People said way back in time, a tiny chapel or chantry once stood on it. This was dedicated to John the Baptist and masses were said there when a member of the landowner's family died, England being a Roman Catholic country at the time. But when I looked at the little island, all I could see was a thick layer of weeds and brambles, a scattering of small bushes and a selection of spindly trees. I could not see any trace of a little chapel anywhere.

The Colney Park estate had an interesting history. Several wealthy local families, the Cheduits, the Fitz Reiners, the De Mandevilles and the Pulteneys, had all owned the land at some point. The Pulteneys built the first "big house". Its original name, Colney Chapel, was, perhaps, chosen as a reminder of the tiny chantry on the island. Later, the "big house", after being enlarged and rebuilt several times, was rechristened Colney Park, adding "Park" to the name of a "big house" being thought the fashionable thing to do at the time, if it had a bit of open land around it.

Over the years, other owners or tenants of the estate included a former Governor of Madras, Charles Boudries, and an Earl of Kingston. Eventually, Patrick Haddow, a High Sheriff of Hertfordshire, bought it and passed it on to Sir Andrew Lusk. He went on to become Lord Mayor of London. Sir Andrew sold it on, in turn, to Mr Kingham, my father's employer. But when I was about five or six years old, the "big house" and its land changed hands yet again and this time the people who bought it were totally different from any who had been connected with it previously.

The new owners were an Anglican order of nuns. Its full title was The Society of All Saints' Sisters of the Poor. It was not an enclosed one. The nuns worked in the outside world caring for the old and the sick. For the fifty years their Order had been in existence, they had been based in three houses in Margaret Street in London. At first just five or six nuns lived there with their Mother Foundress, a Miss Harriet Brownlow Byron. But their order flourished and very soon it was providing nursing staff for University College Hospital in the capital. In time, branches were opened elsewhere in the country and others established overseas, in South Africa, India and North and South America. One of its nuns helped found the first training school for nurses in the United States. The Order now needed a much larger place for its central headquarters.

The nuns demolished the existing "big house" on the Colney Park estate and erected in its place a brand new

"Mother House", which they called All Saints Convent. I have been given to understand it was built in neo-Tudor style to a design by Leonard Stokes, a well-known architect and, as it happened, a Roman Catholic. I can just recall standing watching teams of horses straining to haul heavy wagonloads of bricks up to the site. It was about two years before the Convent was finished. But the nuns moved in gradually as the various parts were finished. They asked my father to plant an avenue of poplar trees along their new wide drive that led straight from the front gate to the main door. They were a splendid sight when fully grown.

John Betjeman, the famous poet, is said to have called the new Convent, "one of the best pieces of modern gothic" when he saw it for the first time. To me, it just seemed an exciting, different sort of place. I loved the patterns traced on its outer walls with red and purple bricks and the eye-catching rows of small windows. But the tall square tower, rising high above the main door, impressed me most. The communal rooms and stone-flagged cloisters were all on the ground floor. The cloisters opened on to a pleasant courtyard with a lawn in the centre. The nuns seemed to spend a lot of time walking round these. Their own individual private rooms were on the first floor.

In time, I came to know certain parts of the Convent, such as the dairy, quite well. Also the infirmary, which the nuns called the lazaret. A constant stream of patients were brought in from outside for the nuns to nurse.

The Convent did not have a proper church. The nuns could not afford to build both a Convent and a church at the same time. A magnificent one, almost a miniature cathedral, designed by another famous architect, Ninian Comper, was added two decades later. Until that time services were held in the Great Hall, the Convent's refectory. Dr Festing, the Anglican Archbishop of St Albans, presided over the opening ceremony in there. The nuns, meanwhile, used a room on the ground floor as a private chapel for their own daily private prayers.

To me, the nuns' arrival seemed to have little effect on my family. My father continued to work as Bailiff and we carried on living in our cottage, although now he worked and we lived on the All Saints estate. The Convent bell was the thing I noticed most at first. It rang every day at seven in the morning, again at noon, then once more at six in the evening, alerting all the Sisters to the fact it was time for prayers. Vespers was what the nuns said. Although I soon became so used to the sound of the bell, I scarcely heard it at all.

None of the estate workers' children were allowed to play near the "big house". That same rule applied to the new Convent. But I began to come across the Sisters as I wandered round the estate, and I always found them most friendly and kind. As far as I am aware, they behaved this way towards all the workers' children they met.

However, once they had settled in, the nuns did make some changes. Cattle and pigs were introduced to the estate. The cattle would supply all the milk they needed and any surplus could be made into butter and cheese in their own dairy, while the pigs, fattened up and sold, would bring in a small income. As it happened, my father was particularly successful with the new animals. So successful, he decided to enter them in the local agricultural shows. These were held quite frequently and were great social occasions. Local Head Gardeners and Bailiffs were keen to display their produce and stock. The shows were an opportunity for them to meet up with each other and pass on bits of gossip about life on the estates where they worked.

On the surface, they all seemed friendly enough. But, underneath, there was real competition between them. The exhibits were entered under the estate owners' names, Sir This and Lady That or Mr So-and-So. But everyone knew who was really responsible for seeing they were up to show standard. A first prize brought with it considerable prestige. A few such successes might help an ambitious Head Gardener or Bailiff get a better-paid job on a bigger estate. My father won cup after cup with his magnificent shorthorn cattle and his splendid pigs, White Yorkshires and Berkshire Blacks.

A few years after the nuns arrived, they provided my family with a special little luxury that I thought was the best change of all. They had water piped into our cottage. A small pump house had pumped water from a well into the former "big house". Now up to two hundred people would be living in the Convent, so a much bigger pump house had to be built. And it was big enough to supply us with water, too. The nuns had a lovely new cooking range installed in our kitchen. It had an oven on one side of the fire like our old one. But the new one also had a large copper fixed to the other. Cold water was piped straight into the copper and heated by the fire. Then we drew off the hot water through a tap at the bottom. The nuns seemed very keen we should have a supply of hot water to wash ourselves.

I have no idea why the nuns chose the Colney Park estate as the site for their new Convent. There could have been many reasons. But I have often wondered whether the one thing that influenced them above any other was the fact that a tiny chapel was said to have once stood on the little island, meaning a fragment of land was already consecrated ground. Although it is possible they knew nothing of the little chapel's existence until they arrived.

Some time after the Order was fully installed in the Convent, two of the nuns, Sister Clare Christine and Sister Elspeth, began to thumb through all the old documents. Then they started to search Chantry Island. They hacked away at the undergrowth and dug holes here and there until, one day, almost by chance, they unearthed traces of the little chapel's foundations. They arranged for the area that had been the tiny chapel's original floor to be completely cleared of vegetation and concrete flagstones were laid there. Finally, a small stone altar was erected at one end.

Every year after that, on the twenty-fourth of June, the Feast Day of John the Baptist, all of us — the nuns, the estate workers and their families — used to form a grand procession. We walked from the Convent, crossed the little wooden bridge that went over the stream and stood on the flagstones while a service was held there.

CHAPTER
THREE

Looking back now, I think I had a very happy and contented childhood. I cannot remember a time when I was either bored or lonely. I always had Stanley and Alice to keep me company. The three of us were content to amuse ourselves. The grown-ups expected it of us.

We could roam freely over most of the estate. And we did not hesitate to trespass on neighbouring ones. There was no lack of open spaces if we wanted to kick a ball about. The three of us played many an exciting game of hide and seek in the woods. They provided endless trees for us to climb and swing from. Sometimes we stood in the doorway of the new pump house, fascinated by the rattling machinery inside. Because we were the Bailiff's children we were allowed to have our own horses. None of the other workers' children could have them. So we spent a lot of time on these, riding up and down the lanes. And we did not have to look after them ourselves. The workers on the estate took care of them for us.

But I think in many ways my parents were very strict with us. For instance, we used to wear our best shoes to school, but the minute we came home we had to change into our old ones. And then set to and clean our best ones, so they were ready, bright and shiny, for the next morning. My mother always inspected them to see we had done the job to her satisfaction before we were allowed out to play.

On Saturday mornings, the three of us had our own special jobs to do. Mine was to clean the outside of our big copper kettle, blackened with a week's soot from the kitchen fire. First I smeared the juice of half a lemon over it. Then applied ample quantities of "Bluebell", a popular patent cleaner. It took a lot of time and elbow grease to work up the final gleaming finish my mother expected.

Meanwhile, Stanley was scrubbing away at the outsides of the saucepans. And very black they were too. For the past week we had cooked our food in them over the open fires. At the same time Alice was busy sweeping and scrubbing the floors in the dining room and drawing room. We took it in turns to clean and polish the brass fire irons we used in there. And an excellent job we had to make of them. My mother was a most particular woman as far as our home was concerned. Everything in it always had to be just so. She was an excellent cook and the nuns used to ask her to help in the Convent kitchen when they were short of staff for some reason.

During the week Mrs Rolt, the wife of one of the under-cowmen, came in for two hours a day to help my mother with the housework. As soon as she arrived each morning, she plodded up the stairs carrying a bucket with a lid and emptied the chamber pots. She did all the washing and all the ironing. How she used to puff and pant as she turned the handle of our old mangle. She was paid two shillings a week and given a midday meal.

As a boy, I always looked forward to Saturday, in spite of having to clean our copper kettle. On Saturdays my father gave me my pocket money. It was just one penny, and that one penny had to last me the whole week. But my one penny was worth four farthings and I need spend only one of these at a time. If I wanted some sweets, and I usually did, I walked or cycled to the shop in London Colney about a mile or so away. I remember one of my favourites, a small round piece of toffee stuck on the end of a wooden stick, was called a farthing firelighter. A sherbet sucker was another I often fancied, a bag of sherbet with a hollow liquorice straw inside. Something similar is still on sale in shops today.

However, as I got older, Stanley and myself did not only buy sweets with our pocket money. We used to get a few cigarette papers as well. We would secretly help ourselves to a few strands of father's tobacco from his tin in the cellar, hide away in a corner of a field and try rolling a few cigarettes to smoke. We felt very grown up. But despite much practice, we never became very expert.

There was another occasion when Stanley and I misbehaved. As with the incident at the well, we did something our parents had endlessly forbidden us not to do. And again water was involved.

My parents were very worried about the little stream on the other side of the field next to our cottage. They had warned all three of us never to play near it. But, as with the well, our parents' disapproval only increased the stream's attraction for Stanley and me. Why is it that children, on being told not to do something by their parents, so often seem compelled to go and do it? Secretly, we set to and collected all the old pieces of wood we could find. We spent hours nailing them together and, in the end, we succeeded. We had made ourselves a raft. It was a very crude raft, but were we proud of it, when we had finished.

There was just one snag. We had to keep the raft hidden away behind a small group of bushes. And when we tried to drag it from its hiding place we made a totally unforeseen discovery. Because of all the wood we had used, the raft was very heavy, far too heavy for just Stanley and me to move. So we had to ask sister Alice to help. This she did willingly.

Together, the three of us managed to drag the raft over to the stream. Gleefully, we watched it slide into the narrow stretch of water surrounding Chantry Island. Having helped us to launch it, Alice now expected to join us on board. It really was only a very small raft, so small there was scarcely enough room for two. Definitely not enough for three. So we had to say no. Was Alice cross! Off she ran home and told our parents what we were up to. Of course, they came rushing over at once. And that was the end of our trip on the water. And our raft. As we expected, Stanley and I got a good hiding from my father for our disobedience.

Fortunately, there were a few diversions to help keep my mind off further mischief. Sometimes my parents took the three of us for a ride on an open-topped bus in St Albans. This was considered a very special treat. And, occasionally, I was allowed to go with one of the men to fetch "grains" from Adey and White, a firm of brewers, in St Albans. The "grains" were fed to the animals in winter. We used to take a large cart drawn by Nobby, a big bay horse. The "grains" were always steaming hot when we collected them. Sitting on the front of the cart with them piled high up behind me, I could feel their heat on my back all the way home.

As I got older, the men used to let me go with them on their regular sparrow hunts. All they needed was a big piece of net. It had to have a very fine mesh and a thin strip of wood attached to either end to weigh it down. They used to creep quietly along holding the strips of wood in their hands. Then, suddenly, they would throw the net over any bush or small tree where they thought the sparrows were hiding. The ivy clinging to the walls of our house regularly yielded dozens.

Once the birds were trapped, there was no escape. The men carefully extracted them from the net, one by one, and expertly crushed each neck between a thumb and forefinger. Then all the little bodies were packed in big bags and taken back to their cottages. There, they made a small nick in the breast of each bird with a sharp knife and ripped off the whole of the outer layer of skin and feathers at one go. Next head, claws and tiny gullet were removed. Thirty or forty birds, packed tightly together under a thick pastry crust, made a very tasty "sparrow pie". No-one ever suggested it was cruel to kill the sparrows. Country folk simply looked on them as a free supply of food.

Whatever the weather or season the men working on the estate always seemed to have plenty to do. They did a twelve-hour day from six o'clock in the morning until six at night, except for Saturdays, when they finished at four. They had only one break, from twelve until one, for their lunch. I remember noticing they always began to work just that little bit more slowly as they listened for the noon vesper bell. Tools were downed immediately the first dong sounded.

The men did not get any proper regular holidays, except at such times as Easter and Christmas. So there was no going away to distant places for a week or two each year. And having to work on Saturdays meant there was not much chance of even a weekend away either. Most people stayed put for most of the time. Although I remember we once had an outing to the Isle of Wight. My father paid for all the estate workers to go. Why he did, I do not know.

If the men were sick, they did not get any pay. No work, no money. It was as simple as that. No-one expected anything different. I never heard anyone grumble about it. Most of them took the precaution of paying a copper or two each week to one of the Friendly Societies. They acted as a kind of insurance company, paying the men something when they were ill, plus a small sum towards their medical expenses.

My father belonged to the Ancient Order of Foresters. He held some formal position with them, which entitled him to wear a special uniform. Sometimes he rode on a horse in processions in St Albans, wearing it.

I remember, each year, my father used to celebrate his birthday in style. All the estate workers and their families were invited to a party in the big barn. Waiting for them was a feast of turkey, chicken, jelly and trifle. In return, the workers had a collection among themselves and gave my father a present. I remember, once, it was a chairman's gavel.

For most of the time, the grown-ups, like the children, had to devise their own entertainment to fill what leisure hours they had. Whist drives and musical evenings were very popular. People took it in turns to open up their home and provide prizes and refreshments. Many an evening I have seen both our dining room and drawing room crammed with people playing cards. On musical evenings almost everyone contributed something, a song, a poem or a short solo on a musical instrument. My mother and Alice used to play the piano. I had a go on the fiddle. But, for some reason, Stanley refused to do anything at all. Everyone seemed to have a good time. Looking back now, I think it was because they were determined to enjoy themselves.

Three or four times a year, at least, a travelling fair used to come to London Colney. There was tremendous excitement whenever one arrived, among the grown-ups as well as the children. Everyone went to them. They consisted mostly of sideshows and stalls, such as hoop-la and coconut shies and ones where you threw darts for prizes. There might be one or two mechanical rides for the grown-ups, but always some for the children. These were worked by hand. The man in charge stood in the centre gripping a handle on a big wheel. He had to give the wheel a good hard push to get the roundabout started. But once it was underway, it carried on going round by itself. When the ride was over he gradually stopped the wheel turning and brought the roundabout to a halt.

Then the fairs began to bring along a new attraction: Cinematograph shows. They were a sensation. I had to queue for a long time outside the big tent and it cost a whole penny to get in to see them. A whole week's pocket money for me. But I did not begrudge it one bit. Like everyone else, I was fascinated by the shows.

Inside the tent there was only a very small screen with a piano next to it. Usually, a woman played the piano. The films had no soundtrack, so she played music to suit the mood of whatever scene was being shown on the screen at the time. Something slow and mournful if it were a sad scene. Something faster and livelier if the actors were rushing about. And they usually were. Most of the films were comedies of the knockabout kind, where the actors threw themselves about and did all sorts of amazing stunts. The audiences loved every minute. They never stopped laughing during the whole of the show. I can remember hearing them as I stood queuing outside the tent. I could not wait to get inside and see the film for myself.

CHAPTER
FOUR

Gradually, I saw less of Alice. As she got older, she had to stay indoors more and more to help my mother in the house. But Stanley and I continued to roam the estate together and we got to know some of the men, who worked there, very well

All three of us knew Mr Bricknell, the Head Cowman, because he called at our cottage every morning. Usually, he had one of the under-cowmen with him. Both men balanced enormous wooden yokes across their shoulders. These had a chain dangling from each end. The chains were attached to enormous buckets filled to the brim with milk. The men were taking the milk over to the Convent's dairy. Mr. Bricknell would dip his big ladle into one of the buckets and carefully transfer our day's supply into my mother's jug. We got our milk free as part of my father's wages. And a generous amount it was, too. The buckets must have been very heavy, but some days, the two of them had to make several journeys, with the buckets full to the brim each time.

Stanley and I thought up our own "special" names for some of the estate workers, especially those we came across most often. We christened the two under-gardeners "May and Blossom", because wherever one of them happened to be working, the other one always seemed to be working close by. We gave the name "Doddles" to the man who did all the odd jobs on the estate, because he was always "doddling" about. One of the under-cowmen we called "Dicky Bird", for no particular reason, just that the name appealed at the time. Both of us liked poor old Dicky Bird. Today some people might call him one of life's "innocents", although we did not realise that was the case until we were much older.

Like boys everywhere, Stanley and myself could make thorough nuisances of ourselves on occasions. I am ashamed to say we did this more often than some. We knew the estate workers would not readily complain as often or as loudly as they might, because we were the Bailiff's children. One little trick particularly appealed to us. We played it over and over again. Usually on the same few people. Now, I can appreciate what an annoyance it must have been for them. We would tie a length of cotton to the knocker on the front door of one of the worker's cottages, then hide close by and pull hard on the other end. This made the knocker rat-tat loudly on the door. Of course the people living there thought they had a visitor and went to the trouble of opening it. How we chortled as they stepped outside and looked and looked around, annoyed to find nobody there.

One day, the two of us thought up an extra special lark. An exciting variation on our usual knocker trick. It was to be inflicted on poor old Dicky Bird, one of our most frequent victims. Absorbed in our plotting neither of us considered we might be planning a potential catastrophe.

It happened like this. Quite by chance, we discovered Dicky Bird's wife had gone away for a few days to visit relatives, so he was alone in his home. The next day, while he was still out working on the estate, we climbed on the roof of his tiny cottage and lowered a big tin, with a heavy brick inside, half way down his chimney. We held it there with a length of string tied to the handle. The string, stretched taut, went up the chimney, down the roof and across to a small tree nearby. The other end of the string we wrapped round its trunk. Then, hidden behind some bushes next to the tree, we waited and waited for Dicky Bird to come home.

It was dark by the time he appeared. Once he was indoors, we silently watched him through the window. He carefully lit a well-stoked fire, sat down in front of it and ate his supper from a bowl. When he had finished, he put the bowl on the floor and took up his favourite position. As we knew he would. This was not the first time we had secretly watched Dicky Bird relaxing in his cottage. Pulling his armchair even closer to the fire, he lay right back in it. Then, lifting his legs, he spread them wide and placed one foot on either end of the low mantelpiece. His rear end, our bull's-eye, was now poised in exactly the right position.

At once, we cut the string with a knife. And sent the weighted tin crashing down on the roaring fire.

Immediately, a cascade of bright sparks and fragments of burning wood and coal spurted into the room, most of them homing straight in on our target, poor old Dicky Bird's backside. Fortunately, the few that missed did not appear to do any damage.

I have to admit now that in playing such a trick, our behaviour went beyond the reckless. It merited the classification of downright dangerous. The only excuse I can offer is that at the time, both of us were still quite young. And the excitement generated by what we thought was our own cleverness, totally blacked out any thoughts of potential risk.

However, Stanley and I were not the only ones to play tricks on poor old Dicky Bird. Some of the grown-ups did, too. I remember George Cato, the senior gardener, playing one particular joke on him.

One evening George climbed a tree and wedged a large bucket, filled with cold water, across two branches. Quite a few of the men and their wives stood and watched. They had guessed something amusing was about to happen. When Dicky Bird arrived, George called down to him. He pretended he had spotted an owl's nest and suggested Dicky Bird should walk under the branches of the tree to see if he could spot the nest, too. But when he did walk under the branches and look up, George poured the bucket of cold water over him. Dicky Bird's clothes were soaked. Everyone watching laughed and laughed, thinking the episode enormous fun.

When Stanley and I were in our early teens, my father bought us a gun, a .22 rifle to be shared between us. We were only allowed to have our rifle because we were the Bailiff's sons. Apart from my father, none of the other workers were allowed to have a gun and shoot on the estate. To our delight, we found quite a few people were prepared to give us a little something for the occasional pheasant or brace of wild duck. I'm ashamed to confess we were not deterred from poaching some from neighbouring estates. Surprisingly, there were very few rabbits about at the time.

But yet again, trouble beckoned Stanley and me. We were forbidden to use our rifle on the Sabbath. But one particular Sunday we longed desperately for some extra shooting practice. I do not remember now whether we just hoped no-one would see or hear us. Or whether we realised they might and yet were still keen enough to take that risk. But we decided pigeons would make an ideal target. So very, very quietly and very, very slowly, we crept into a group of cedar trees on the far side of the enormous lawn, behind the Convent. We reckoned we had a good chance of spotting a few of the birds there.

However, unbeknown to us, Stanley and I were not the only ones to seek the seclusion of the cedar trees that afternoon. Sister Clare, the Convent's beekeeper, was sitting on a bench, behind one of them, quite close to us. Meditation and prayer was probably her way of passing that particular Sunday afternoon. So it was likely she was totally unaware of what was going on around her. She certainly did not expect Stanley and me to be there, with or without our rifle.

Taking aim at a fat pigeon we fired off our first shot. Instantly, we heard Sister Clare scream at the top of her voice. Naturally, we rushed over to her at once. Just in time to see her slide slowly off the bench and lie flat on her back on the ground. Dramatically she raised an arm. Pointed an accusing finger at us. And shrieked that we had shot her. For one long, dreadful moment, we really thought we had. Fortunately, we had not. We had just given her a good fright that was all.

But what could Stanley and I say? First, we knew we were not supposed to be in that particular spot on a Sunday, even without a gun. Second, we knew we were forbidden to take our gun anywhere at all on the Sabbath. The fact was we had risked taking our gun out with us and had then dared to go in among the cedar trees with it. Above all, we had been so determinedly self-willed as actually to fire it on the most sacred day of the week. All this, taken together, could be looked on as signs of total unforgivable, depravity. Neither of us uttered a word. There were no explanations. There were no excuses.

But sometimes miracles do happen. I think one must have happened that day.

Even now, looking back, I still think of it as a miracle. Stanley suddenly spotted a dead rat lying at the foot of one of the cedar trees. I cannot understand why we had not noticed it before. But, somehow, Stanley happened to spot it at that exact moment. Talking about it afterwards, it seemed to both of us, just like a miracle the rat should happen to be there.

Stanley told Sister Clare the noise she had heard was the two of us shooting the rat. Rats were a real pest at the time. Sister Clare was delighted there was now one less. So delighted, she immediately marched us into the Convent and into the office of the Mother Superior, Sister Mary Augustine, who rewarded us with a handful of bulls-eyes. She always kept a few to give to the children on the estate. I always had a special high regard for Sister Mary Augustine. She seemed to me to have a particularly sweet and gentle nature. Some people said she was a descendant of Lord Nelson, but I have no idea whether this was actually so.

However, my father had not given Stanley and me the rifle solely for our amusement. At the time he was rearing a lot of young turkeys. The nuns hoped these would bring in a little extra money when they were sold at Christmas. The young turkeys were kept in big open pens and they attracted scores of jackdaws. The birds were a real menace. They would continually swoop down and peck, peck, peck away at the young turkey's heads. The baby turkeys were terrified. They would scatter wildly everywhere trying to keep out of reach, but they were trapped by the sides of the pen. The jackdaws kept at them all day long, digging their sharp beaks further and further into the heads of the birds they had injured, killing some and leaving others in such a bad way they did not survive the night. Day after day this was happening. So my father told Stanley and me to build ourselves a hide near the pen. From there, we were to use our gun to fire at the jackdaws as soon as they appeared, maybe killing a few but, more importantly, scaring the rest away.

We did exactly as our father instructed. And we were reasonably successful. But, after a few days, simply shooting a handful of jackdaws, one at a time, no longer satisfied us. Oh no. Stanley and I had a much bigger idea. Once again, like all youngsters beguiled by a belief in their own cleverness, we abandoned any thoughts of prudence. By now we were used to our gun. To us, a gun was a weapon that meant danger, even death. But only for certain carefully chosen wild creatures. We gave no thought to the fact that, given a slight twist in fortune, the same might be said of it in relation to ourselves.

My father had a twelve-bore shotgun. We boys knew under no circumstances would he ever lend this to either of us. So we were not about to ask him to loan it to us. Nor would we risk borrowing it without his permission. We suspected if we begged for a handful of his cartridges he would not give them to us either. So we thought we would be very clever. We decided we would not bother to ask him. Or even mention to him what we were thinking of doing. We would simply quietly help ourselves.

We knew where he kept his cartridges. Hidden away in the cellar under the stairs. So, secretly, we went in there, got a handful and quietly transferred them to our hide near the turkeys. Very carefully we opened up one or two of the cartridges and removed the powder and shot. Then we opened up one of our own cartridges and removed the powder and shot from that. Next, we put our empty cartridge into the breech of our rifle and poured the powder and shot from my father's cartridges into the barrel. Ramming it down as hard as we could. We were really ready for the jackdaws now.

Soon, the jackdaws began to swoop down low over the young turkeys again. We had already agreed Stanley would have first go. So he fired, killing two of them straight off. But even two birds at a time were still not enough. Determined to better that score, we began to reload our gun, deciding to put in double the quantity of powder and shot from my father's cartridges into the barrel. And we rammed it down even harder. We were both cock-a-hoop. We had a really powerful weapon now.

How excited the two of us were as we waited for the jackdaws to come again. Now we were fully prepared. We had a proper welcome for them. Within minutes, a new group arrived and began to bombard the young turkeys. This time, it was my turn to fire. Carefully, I held the rifle up to my right eye, took aim and pressed the trigger. I heard the extra loud bang quite clearly. But I could not see whether I had killed any birds. In fact, I could not see anything at all. Blood had filled both my eyes and was overflowing down my cheeks. The gun had exploded in my face.

Stanley had to lead me back home, very slowly. I have never forgotten feeling how much his hand was trembling as it rested on my arm. My mother sent for the doctor right away. She was certain I had lost the sight of at least one eye, if not both. But I was very fortunate indeed. As it happened, neither of my eyes was permanently affected. But to this day, I still have two small scars to remind me of this incident, one over my right eye and another on my right thumb. Stanley and I were not allowed to have our rifle after that.

CHAPTER
FIVE

When I was a boy, Sunday was kept very strictly indeed. It was a real "Sabbath Day". No-one went to work. All the shops were closed. Only the most essential jobs were done on the estate, such as milking. At the special request of the Mother Superior, Sister Augustine, no cooking or housework of any sort was ever done on that day. All our Sunday meals were prepared on the Saturday and eaten cold.

As far as we children were concerned, recreation of any sort was banned on Sundays. So it was a very quiet day for us indeed, with the hour after our Sunday lunch being the quietest hour of all. This was the time my father always had his afternoon nap, stretched out in his favourite armchair drawn up close to the drawing room fire if it were chilly, a large, clean, white handkerchief draped over his face. If any of us dared to make the slightest sound while he was asleep, he made us stand in the corner with our faces to the wall.

On Sunday, almost all the local families went to church at least once, dressed up in their Sunday best clothes. These were never worn on any other day of the week. Both men and women always had hats and gloves and most carried their own Bible and prayer book.

Usually, everyone attended the services at their local parish church. Before the Convent was built, my mother and father went to the one in the tiny hamlet of Shenleybury, the church there being the nearest one to the estate. Most people walked. But, I believe, at one time, the church had a big open shed nearby where people who did ride or drive could leave their horses. A few, like my parents, used a small pony and trap. The local "gentry" always arrived in a four-wheeled brougham, driven by a groom. He waited outside during the service and kept an eye on the two horses.

My family always attended church twice on Sundays. It is a habit I have kept up all my life. After the Convent was built, all the estate workers and their families went to the Sunday services held there in the Great Hall, one at nine o'clock in the morning and another at six in the evening. They lasted about an hour. Then for Stanley, Alice and me, there was another half an hour of Sunday School in the Convent, from eleven thirty until noon. Children who attended this regularly could expect two special treats. Once a year, we were allowed to climb to the top of the convent tower. From there, we had a wonderful view across the fields towards Radlett, Shenley and St Albans. And every summer we had a party. The same routine was followed each time. First, we chased each other up and down the big lawn at the back of the Convent, trying to be the winner of various races. Then played game after game until, exhausted, we headed for the shade of the cedar trees (the same trees where Stanley and I would have our encounter with Sister Clare). Waiting for us was an enormous tea of sandwiches and cake. We all had a wonderful time.

The Great Hall was always full for both Sunday services. All the nuns were present. Those wearing long black robes, white headbands and long black veils hanging down their backs were full sisters of the Order. They sat at the front. Behind them sat the lay sisters. They were preparing to become full members. Their outfits were similar but a pale grey colour. Behind the lay Sisters sat about fifty orphans. They lived at the Convent in the care of the nuns. Seated at the back behind the orphans were the estate workers and their families, plus any local people from outside the estate who chose to attend the services.

The services could be described as very "high church". My father carried the cross. When Stanley and I were old enough, we acted as servers with four other boys from the estate. Sometimes, during services marking special events in the Christian calendar such as those held at Easter, we led the congregation all round the cloisters in a grand procession.

But there were two types of services which were special private ones. None of the estate workers, their families or any outsiders were allowed to attend them. They were held in the nuns' own small private chapel. I was present only because I acted as a server.

A special private service was arranged when a lay sister was admitted to full membership of the Order. Or "took the veil" as it was usually known. Although these were solemn occasions, there was always a festive atmosphere in the chapel. The nuns seemed especially happy. Genuinely delighted to be welcoming a newcomer.

The lay sister or apostolate being admitted to the order entered the chapel dressed just like a bride. She wore a long, flowing white dress and her face was hidden by a lovely, delicate, white, lace veil. Two full sisters of the Order, one walking either side of her, escorted her to the altar. Father Fowler, the Convent's resident priest, officiated. He lived in a small cottage next to the estate's main gate. The service was the same as that for a wedding ceremony, the apostolate vowing to be obedient and faithful to God and Father Fowler putting a gold ring on her finger as a sign she was now a "Bride of Christ". At a certain point during the second half of the service, she withdrew from the chapel. When she reappeared a short while later, she was dressed in the black robes of a full Sister, the uniform she would wear for the rest of her natural life. The new nun also put aside the name given to her in the outside world. From then on, she would only be known as Sister followed by her newly adopted Saint's name. Whether she chose this herself or whether the Mother Superior chose it for her, I have no idea.

This type of service, the admission of a lay sister to the Order, took place frequently when I was a boy. Although I was only young at the time, those "taking the veil" appeared to me to be quite young, too, either in their late teens or early twenties, as near as I could judge. Looking back now, I am still surprised so many well-educated and, I thought, attractive young ladies from wealthy backgrounds decided to leave their families to follow such an austere way of life.

The new nuns did not stay long at the Convent. Just long enough to finish their training. Usually it was linked to some type of nursing care. Then they were sent elsewhere, to wherever they were most needed. Sometimes they stayed in this country. Sometimes they went abroad. Meanwhile those Sisters who had become too old or too ill to go on working in the outside world were returning to the Convent to spend whatever time they had left to them.

The other private service I attended as a server took place after one of the nuns died. The same ritual was followed each time. The previous evening, my father and three other estate workers carried the coffin containing the body of the dead nun into the small chapel and placed it on a stand in front of the altar. Two tall oak candlesticks were put at the head of the coffin and two others at the feet. Then a large candle was placed in each of them. These were special, expensive candles. The wax was not white. It was a browny yellow colour. The coffin was not left alone after that. Some of the nuns watched and prayed over it, in turn, throughout the night.

Next morning, after the funeral service had ended, my father and three estate workers carried the coffin out of the chapel. They took it to a special section of the convent's grounds close by, which they used as their burial ground. My father had seen to it the grave was dug ready. All the nuns watched as the coffin was lowered into it and covered with earth. Finally, a small wooden cross, giving the name of the nun and the date of her death, was placed in the ground.

One particular incident, connected with the death of a nun, has stuck in my mind. I must have been about ten years old at the time, maybe a little older, but definitely no more than twelve. One of the nuns had died and my father asked me to go with him to collect her coffin. When a nun died a special coffin was ordered from somewhere in London. It came by train to Radlett station. Two pairs of hands were needed for the job but the man who usually went with him wasn't available that afternoon, for some reason.

My father and I drove to the station in a pony and trap. We found the coffin waiting for us when we got there. It was an expensive coffin. All the nuns' coffins were. It was beautifully made of solid oak, with a set of shiny brass handles along each side. It was very heavy and very big. So big we had to lower the tailboard of the trap, then lay the coffin across it, pushing it forward until a section was wedged under the seat.

When we got back to the Convent, the two of us just managed to carry the coffin into the lazaret. One of the Sisters was inside, waiting with the body of the dead nun. As she and my father stood ready to transfer the corpse to the coffin, he asked me if I would do something to help them. I wonder now whether he did so as a bit of a joke. But perhaps not. The dead nun's body was lying on a bed, covered with a white sheet. My father suggested it would help if I removed this. So I pulled the sheet aside. And discovered, to my horror,

40

the long black veil the nuns wore did not conceal hair, as I had always imagined, but a closely shaven skull.

As I lived on the estate, I regularly came in contact with quite a few of the nuns. Especially those who formed the Convent's permanent staff. Each was responsible for a particular set of essential day-to-day tasks which helped to ensure the smooth running of the Convent.

One of these nuns I remember particularly well. Her name was Sister Etheldreda. She was a big woman. Fat actually. She had the sort of build most people would describe as "motherly". And like many women of her size, she was always very lively and jolly. Sister Etheldreda acted as the Convent's Bursar. She was responsible for seeing there was a regular supply of all the everyday things the nuns needed, any extra food, cleaning materials, medicines, etc. She used to drive into St Albans quite regularly, almost every week in fact, to order whatever goods were required from the shops there.

Sister Etheldreda went to St Albans in a horse and chaise, a four-wheeled carriage with room for four people. She must have felt the need for some company on these trips, because she always called at our cottage and asked either Stanley or me to go with her. And whoever went was always given a small, silver sixpenny piece to spend in the town. An instant fortune to someone who only had one penny for his weekly pocket money.

The sixpences were taken from Sister Etheldreda's own private supply of money, not from Convent funds.

The nuns renounced all worldly possessions when they took their vows. So none of them were supposed to have any money of their own. But, like most of the nuns, Sister Etheldreda came from a wealthy family. It seemed they kept sending her cheques, even after she became a full Sister of the Order. Whether she asked them to do this, I never knew. But it meant Sister Etheldreda had a private personal problem. She needed to get the cheques cashed. She could not change them in the shops in St Albans in case news of her secret wealth got back to the Convent. So she used to slip them to my father. He acted as her banker. He cashed her cheques and kept a store of money for her. Then he quietly handed over to her whatever amount she needed, whenever she needed it.

What did Sister Etheldreda buy with her money? I am not quite sure. Stanley and I were always given our sixpence and told to go off and spend it. Perhaps she did this so we would not see what she was buying. But I have an idea she bought expensive toilet soap and nice lace handkerchiefs. And I have also got an impression, from somewhere or other, she bought herself some pretty underwear.

Stanley and I puzzled and puzzled over her. What could have made such a naturally happy, friendly person as Sister Etheldreda abandon her home and become a nun. We talked about it and we talked about and we talked about it. Until after much pondering, in our innocence, we came to the only conclusion we thought made any sense. We decided she must have been crossed in love. This may or may not have been the truth. We never knew.

Looking back now, I sometimes wonder whether Sister Etheldreda's calling at our cottage to pick up either Stanley or me was just a cover. But she did seem genuinely fond of us both. And we were very fond of her. We would willingly have gone with her to St Albans, even without the offer of the sixpence. Like the rest of my family, I continued to have a very high regard for all the Sisters, despite knowing Sister Etheldreda's little secret.

I received my first few years of schooling at the Convent. The nuns started a school and the estate workers' children were invited to attend. So at the age of five I joined Alice, who was already a pupil. She completed her education there. As it happened, I was the only boy in the class, a situation I thoroughly enjoyed. Both the nuns and the girls were inclined to fuss over me. To be truthful, I rather resented Stanley's arrival three years later. I remember discipline was rigorously enforced in the classroom. And, when necessary, reinforced with a sharp rap across the knuckles with a ruler.

I used a small black slate and a piece of chalk to practise the alphabet and numbers. The lessons had a strong emphasis on reading, writing and basic arithmetic. I do not recall being overburdened with religion, but we did attend a service on every Saints' Day. However, when I reached the age of nine the nuns said I was now too old to be in a class with girls. So I had to transfer to the village school in London Colney, where the boys were taught in one part and the girls in another. I walked there and back each day, taking sandwiches with me for my lunch.

Round about this time I had my first glimpse of the new "horseless carriage" everyone was talking about. Winter was just ending. There had been heavy falls of snow. But the weather was getting a little warmer, so it was melting fast. The result was the River Colne overflowed its banks and flooded a section of the Shenley road running alongside the estate. A man in a car attempted to drive through the water but his engine stalled, leaving him stranded in the middle. Standing watching him do everything he possibly could do to get it restarted, I was not at all impressed by the new invention. I remember thinking a horse would simply have waded straight through.

The River Colne flooded quite regularly and one winter my father almost became one of its victims. A postman, trying to get through the floods on his bike, was swept off a bridge and into the river. My father happened to be nearby, so he jumped in and managed to rescue him. But the sudden shock of entering the icy water almost killed him. Afterwards, he lay prone in bed for over a week. Once or twice, my mother really thought we were about to lose him.

At the age of eleven I moved to the senior school in Shenley, a village about one and a half miles away from the Convent. I attended this for the next two years. I remember the school particularly well because on Oak Apple Day, the twenty-ninth of May, all the boys wore an oak apple in their lapel. Any boy without one had bunches of stinging nettles pressed hard against the backs of his knees. The skin is particularly tender there. Why they were so keen on this tradition I have no idea. Perhaps it was just a good excuse for a bit of playground bullying.

CHAPTER
SIX

Now I had left school, I had my future to consider. I was an ordinary country boy, born and bred, like my father. So it seemed natural I should choose work that was, in some way, connected with the land. That being so, it appeared to me my future career would, inevitably, be linked with the local private country estates. Just as my father's had been.

There were two jobs at the top of the employment ladder to tempt an ambitious worker on a private country estate. They were those of Bailiff and Head Gardener, the difference being that on estates where most of the land was used for farming activities of some sort, it was usual to appoint a Bailiff as the man in charge. While on estates with extensive ornamental flowerbeds or "pleasure gardens" and large greenhouses, a Head Gardener was in control. I knew considerable competition could be expected for both positions. Each had considerable financial and practical advantages attached.

For instance, most married workers on a private country estate were provided with a cottage for their family. But the one allocated to the Head Gardener or Bailiff was usually larger than those given to the other ordinary workers. My family lived very comfortably in our eight rooms. There was also a considerable increase in pay. I do not know exactly how much my father was paid but I believe it was a substantial sum. Plus we had as much free milk and coal as we needed. All the workers on the estate were supplied with free vegetables, but he got eggs and chickens as well. A few poultry were always kept. My father even got the occasional piece of pork. As the Bailiff's son, I was reckoned to be exceptionally well fed. My father was the only worker allowed to have a gun and shoot game on the estate. Stanley and I could have our rifle only because we were the Bailiff's sons.

But I had noticed one other thing connected with my father's top position, which appealed to me above everything else. If you were a Bailiff it meant you were a "somebody". Ordinary folk everywhere, both on the estate and outside it, treated you with respect. All the outdoor staff knew that, as Bailiff, my father had the right to hire and fire any man working under him.

Tradesmen who called were especially deferential. My father spent considerable sums of money on behalf of his employers. Food was needed for the animals, every year quantities of seeds had to be bought, bulbs, shrubs or new trees might have to be planted. I have known all sorts of tradesmen, and what today would be called "sales reps", quietly slip my father a gift of money, you could call it a bribe, to try to make sure he placed an order with them. Some owners of private country estates took a personal interest in such matters, but even then they often listened to and acted on the advice offered by their Head Gardener or Bailiff. Other owners depended totally on them. They gave their Head Gardener or Bailiff complete freedom, usually within some set financial limit, to order everything they thought was needed.

I had my fair share of ambition. Perhaps even a shade more than some people. I saw no reason why I should not work my way up the private country estate employment ladder and eventually hold a position the same or similar to the one my father had. At the time, I saw no reason why private country estates should not provide me with secure employment for the whole of my working life.

My father did everything he could to encourage me. He even suggested some day in the future I might take over his job and become Bailiff on the All Saints estate. Many were the nights I secretly dreamed of doing that. I was confident it would happen. To me, at that time, at my young age, there seemed to be no reason at all why it should not.

But, if I were to stand any chance of fulfilling my aspirations, I had to have the right training and experience. I needed to become familiar with both farming and horticultural procedures. On many estates the Head Gardener or Bailiff was expected to supervise workers engaged on both activities. My father suggested I make a start by working on the All Saints estate. This would give me some experience of the farming side. And what hard work I found the farming side was, too. There were no machines in use in those days. I milked the cows. Every single one of them had to be done by hand. I fed and watered the pigs. Not an easy task. They needed an almost constant supply of water. The water came from a well and I had to keep pump, pump, pumping it by hand into their trough. That almost broke my back.

At harvest time, I walked up and down the fields, up and down the fields, with the rest of the men. Constantly swinging a heavy, long-handled, agricultural scythe from side to side, its long sharp blade slice, slice, slicing through the ripe yellow corn. The women workers followed along behind us, hooking the cut corn towards them with their small sickles so they could bind it up and stack it into "traves", as they were known locally, or stooks as they were called elsewhere. Countless times, I helped mow the huge lawn at the back of the Convent. I used an enormous old mower, so big it needed Nobby, our large bay horse, the same one that used to take me into St Albans, to pull it along. But, first, I had to remember to strap four leather overshoes round his fetlocks, so his hooves did not damage the turf. Then I walked along at the front holding Nobby's head while a man walked at the back guiding the mower.

At the end of two years, my father suggested I should leave farming and concentrate on gardening for a time. Up to now I had not taken much interest in the work of the three gardeners on the estate. My father thought it would be best if I started right at the bottom. I agreed. So he arranged for me to start a three-year apprenticeship with an expert market gardener called Frank Sear.

Frank Sear was not related to my family in any way, despite the similarity in our names. He was a tall man with fair hair but his moustache was a particularly vivid shade of ginger. He and my father were about the same age, round about fifty. The two of them were old friends. In their youth, they had worked alongside each other on a private country estate before their careers had taken them their separate ways. Like my father, Frank Sear had got on in life. He, too, had worked his way up and become a Head Gardener. But when his employer died, Frank decided to leave estate work and set up his own horticultural business. At the time, as a gesture of goodwill, my father gave him a lovely little donkey. I remember it had an exceptionally clear black "cross" marked on its back. The donkey was a most acceptable present from Frank Sear's point of view. It could pull a little cart, loaded with produce, for delivery to his customers.

Despite their long friendship, Frank Sear and my father complied with all the traditional formalities when arranging my apprenticeship. First, my father paid him for the privilege of him taking me on as a pupil. I have no idea how much but it must have been a reasonable sum. And formal indentures were signed. I still have them as a matter of fact.

Looked at today they make rather quaint reading. "This indenture witnesseth that John Sears doth put himself apprentice to Frank Sear, to learn his Art, Trade or Business with him, after the manner of an apprentice". It goes on to say among other things that, "the said Apprentice his Master faithfully shall serve, his secrets keep, his lawful commands everywhere gladly do. He shall do no damage to his said Master nor see it to be done of others. But to the best of his power shall prevent or forthwith give warning to his said Master of the same. He shall not waste the goods of his Master or lend them unlawfully to any. He shall not do any act whereby his said Master may have any loss with his own goods or others. He shall neither buy nor sell nor absent himself from his said Master's service day or night unlawfully. But in all things as a faithful Apprentice, he shall behave himself towards his said Master. And the said Frank Sear shall do all in his power to learn the said Apprentice in the Art, Trade or Business of a Nurseryman and Gardener, which he does by the best means that he can; and shall teach and instruct or cause to be taught and instructed."

At the bottom of the document is my own rather shaky signature, followed by that of Frank Sear and below his are the signature of my parents, John and Ellen Sears.

CHAPTER
SEVEN

I cycled the two miles to Frank Sear's place each day. I had to be ready to start work sharp at nine o'clock and I stayed until five in the afternoon. My lunch break, from one until two, was the only time I stopped working. My father paid Frank Sear some extra money so I could have a hot meal with him and his wife. As an apprentice I did not earn very much, only half a crown a week.

Frank Sear carried on his business of florist and nurseryman in Hatfield Road, on the outskirts of St Albans. He owned twelve acres of land there and rented forty more a short distance away, in an area known as Fleetville. His advertisement in the local town guide stated he was "prepared to supply Shrubs, Fruit Trees, Standard and Dwarf Roses, Flower and Vegetable Seeds, Bulbs, Herbaceous Plants at Lowest Prices consistent with Good Quality. Cut Flowers, Wreaths, Crosses and Wedding Bouquets. Plant lent on hire. Gardens laid and kept in order. Orders by post promptly attended to".

There were several other apprentices. Two were from Holland. Why they had come all the way over to England to learn horticulture, I never knew. We apprentices were in the care of two foremen. I remember one of them, George Currell, had a habit of speaking sideways out of the corner of his mouth. We loved to imitate him. But only behind his back, of course.

Frank Sear also employed twelve or fourteen men. He hired a few of them out one or two days a week to tend small local gardens or keep family graves tidy. Then there were several young boys. They kept the place generally tidy and did any extra work that might be needed, such as sieving soil for the rest of the staff to use. They also looked after the three horses.

Most of the plants, such as delphiniums, michaelmas daises and polyanthus, were grown out of doors. More flowers, begonias and spiraeas amongst others, plus melons and grapes, were grown in several large greenhouses. Frank Sear had two main outlets for his produce. His own shop, sited at the front of the land in Hatfield Road, and a stall in the open-air market held in St Albans each Saturday.

As an apprentice I was to be taught everything a good gardener needed to know. This meant I had to learn how to grow all kinds of plants from seed or cuttings. I had to know which ones would grow out of doors and which should be kept inside in a greenhouse, which were early or late flowering, and so on. Also, and most important, how often to water them and what quantity of water each needed.

In addition to this practical experience, I had to become familiar with the business side of things. So I regularly served customers in the shop. In fact, that was the first thing Frank Sear asked me to do when I started as an apprentice. Sometimes he took me with him when he went up to Covent Garden in London. He went most Fridays to buy more fresh produce to supplement his own stock for market day. When it was my turn to go I slept at his house on the Thursday night. We had to be up at three next morning and walk to St Albans station in time to get the first early train to London. We returned in the afternoon, again by train, with the goods we had bought stacked in the guard's van. One of the men used to meet us at the station with a horse and wagon.

After we got back, everything we had bought in London, tomatoes, potted plants, bedding plants, cucumbers, was repacked in big wooden crates, ready to be taken to the market next morning. The other men had spent the afternoon packing Frank Sear's own flowers and produce in similar crates.

His market stall was just in front of St Albans Town Hall. Like the other apprentices, I was expected to spend some Saturdays serving behind it, always accompanied by one of the foremen. We arrived at the market very early in the morning and stayed until six in the evening. We ate our midday meal in a small café near the market square. Frank Sear paid for it. The bedding plants we sold cost anything from one penny to half a crown. I remember pansies and polyanthus were particularly popular. Tomatoes went for around three pence a pound, while cucumbers were two or three pence each.

54

I discovered Frank Sear had two particularly lucrative sides to his business. The first was the making and selling of wreaths. His shop was conveniently positioned directly opposite the cemetery gates so there was a steady market for funeral wreaths throughout the year, backed by an insatiable demand for those made of holly during the festive period. Any spare moments we had could always be profitably filled by adding to the supply of wreaths.

The second financially rewarding aspect was his landscape gardening service. There appeared to be an endless queue of wealthy people prepared to hand over considerable amounts of money for the privilege of having him remodel their gardens, or create new ones for them. I remember rose gardens and sunken gardens, in particular, were very popular. But ornamental ponds, fountains and even lakes were often requested. Enquiries about tennis courts and swimming pools were by no means unusual, although he always brought in appropriate experts for this type of work.

Occasionally, Frank Sear took me with him when he visited potential customers in their homes. Often, such a visit could mean a journey of several miles. The two of us used to go on our bikes. His had a three-speed gear attached. Unfortunately mine had not. Something he refused to accept as being a handicap in any way.

I had to listen carefully as the nurseryman discussed details of the landscaping required with his customer, then carefully note the estimated price he gave as to how much it would cost. This "estimating of work" was looked on as a most important part of my training. The average price of most landscaping jobs was between fifty and a hundred pounds. But those costing anything between one hundred and five hundred pounds were by no means rare.

However, life was not all work. I did have some leisure time. But in such a rural area there were few things for a young person my age to do. That was why the village dances were so popular. Everyone went, all the young apprentices, young farmers, shop assistants and servants from the "big houses". Stanley and I used to go together. I have no idea who organised them. Tickets were not particularly cheap. They cost half a crown, a whole week's wages for me.

The dances were held in a big hall in London Colney, usually on a Wednesday evening. They were looked on as being very select. Everyone had to be in proper formal dress or they were not allowed in. I wore black trousers, a black dinner jacket and a white shirt with a black bow tie. And I never arrived at the hall without my dancing shoes tucked under my arm. If I did not change into my special lightweight black dancing shoes, I was not allowed on the dance floor. No black dancing shoes, no dancing. All the men understood that. You had no difficulty buying a pair. All the local shoe shops sold them. And I always wore white gloves. So when I put my arm round a lady's waist, there was no risk of her dress being soiled, should my palm become a little hot and sweaty.

The women, too, always dressed up for the dances. All the ladies wore lovely, long dresses, their best and prettiest. And long white gloves, which went right up their arms past their elbows. They were each given a small card when they arrived. A small pencil was attached to these by a cord. The names of the dances were listed on the card in the order they would be performed that evening. Any gentleman wishing to be the lady's partner for a particular dance wrote his name in the space beside it. There was still an expectation of some sort of formal introduction being necessary before a young man could ask a young lady to dance. But, usually, a request for one was rarely refused.

Nowadays, the dances we did are classed as "Old Tyme". But to us, they were just the usual ones we always danced. No evening was complete unless such favourites as the Lancers or the Waltz Cotillion were included. Any that used waltz steps were especially popular. Most people got up and danced. After all, that was what they were there for. People learnt the steps by watching everyone else do them, then trying to do the same.

The music came from gramophone records, although on special occasions, such as New Year's Eve, we could expect a three-piece band, piano, drum and violin. But at every dance, there was a Master of Ceremonies to invite the gentlemen to take their partners on to the dance floor. And halfway through the evening there was always a short interval when you could sit at a small table and have a drink of tea or coffee. Alcohol in any form was never available.

People walked miles to get to the dances. But quite a few came on their bikes. There was an open space behind the hall where people could park them. The women cycled along with the hems of their long dance dresses pulled up and strapped round their waists, often revealing several inches of long legged white bloomers as they pedalled along. Sometimes these were not always as clean as they might be. But nobody minded. For most people the dances were the high spot of the week. Everyone who went to them was determined to enjoy themselves.

Like everyone else, I thoroughly enjoyed the dances. I have continued to enjoy dancing throughout my life. I have always preferred to go to a dance rather than a public house. Perhaps I have been influenced by my father in this. He never went into a public house for a drink himself and tended to infer it was not a desirable thing to be encouraged in a young man.

CHAPTER
EIGHT

In what seemed like no time at all, my three-year apprenticeship was over. Now I knew such things as the correct way to prune rose bushes and grape vines. I could graft apple trees, disbud and layer carnations. I had learnt the secret of how to pollinate peach trees and tomato plants and could be trusted to manage a greenhouse in the proper manner. In short, I was a fully qualified gardener. This meant I was now eligible to take a job as a journeyman, the first rung on the private country estate employment ladder.

Again my father was able to help me. As I have already indicated, Head Gardeners and Bailiffs had the right to appoint and dismiss their own staff. My father was on particularly friendly terms with a local Head Gardener, aptly named Albert Grubb. He, as it happened, had a vacancy for a good reliable journeyman. My father recommended me to him and I was offered my first job.

Mr Grubb was Head Gardener on a private country estate called Porters Park, positioned on the outskirts of Shenley. I knew the village well, having attended the senior school there. The estate had once been owned by Admiral Lord Howe but Mr Grubb's present employer,

Mr Cecil Frank Raphael, had bought it about six years before from a Mr Michael Paul Grace, the then Lord of the Manor of Shenley.

Porters Park was one of the biggest private country estates in the neighbourhood. It stretched to over a thousand acres. They included exceptionally fine large "pleasure gardens", vast areas of parkland and woodland and a big home farm run entirely independently from the main estate. Mr Raphael lived in the big house with his wife. He had a teenage son who went away to boarding school, and a daughter of twelve, who lived at home and had a governess.

Mr Raphael was one of the richest, if not the richest man, in the area. He was something to do with banking, I believe. He always wore a top hat and frock coat when he went to his office in London. Most mornings, the chauffeur drove him to Radlett station in his Rolls Royce. Mr Raphael kept a large staff both indoors and out. I discovered Porters Park was an exceptionally well-run gentleman's private country estate. At all times, things everywhere were always exactly as they should be.

Mr Grubb, the Head Gardener, had four foremen to help him keep the outdoor side of the estate just as it should be. The job of foreman was the next step up from being a journeyman. The first, foreman "pleasure gardens", had three journeymen working under him. Together, they tended the large formal flowerbeds, the "pleasure gardens", surrounding the "big house". They also looked after two tennis courts, the croquet lawn, the cricket pitch and the large ornamental lake. This was always kept well stocked for the convenience of any house guest who might fancy a spot of fishing. Specialist gardeners called in about once a week to care for the eighteen-hole golf course.

Another, foreman "flowers under glass", was responsible for all the flowering plants grown in the greenhouses. Four journeymen worked alongside him. Because of the great number of carnations grown, one of them, Ernie Thrift, was a carnation expert. He and one of the other journeymen looked after all the flowers in the greenhouses. The remaining two worked mostly on the cucumbers, tomatoes and melons. As these were flowering plants grown in the greenhouses, they were considered to be the responsibility of the foreman "flowers under glass". But the two men also helped out with the flowers when needed.

The third, foreman "fruit under glass", had one journeyman and a young lad or "boy" to help him look after all the fruit grown in the greenhouses, while the fourth, foreman "kitchen garden", worked with three journeymen. They took care of all the fruit and vegetables grown out of doors, in the kitchen garden.

In addition to all these skilled men, four local youths helped out anywhere in the gardens or greenhouses as directed by Mr Grubb. They did such jobs as washing out flowerpots or "crocking" them, that is putting a few small pieces of broken pottery in the bottom of each so they were ready for the foremen and journeymen to use.

Mr Grubb's outdoor staff also included two engineers, who supervised the machinery in the pump house. Water was pumped from there into the "big house" and to a few, not all, of the estate cottages. They also looked after the generator. This supplied electricity to the "big house" and a few of the cottages. Then there were two carpenters. They had two other men as their assistants and together they did all the general repair and maintenance work on the estate. Finally, four gamekeepers, one senior to the other three, ensured a good supply of game was available for Mr Raphael and his guests.

As a member of the outdoor staff, I did not see very much of the people who worked indoors. But I discovered there was a butler. He always dressed in a smart frock coat when on duty. Under him were three footmen, one senior to the other two, although all three wore similar uniforms of dark green trousers and short green jackets. Then there was a housekeeper. She always wore a long black dress. She was in charge of the head housemaid, the under-housemaid and the parlour maid. They all wore long black dresses and small white caps. But the parlour maid's cap was slightly larger, to indicate she was not just an ordinary housemaid. There was a lady's maid to look after Mrs Raphael and a valet who waited on Mr Raphael. The valet tended to keep himself very much to himself. He liked to give the impression he was a gentleman's son, who had fallen on hard times. Perhaps he was, perhaps he was not. I had no way of knowing. The kitchen staff consisted of a cook, a kitchen maid and two laundry maids.

Then there were two chauffeurs, one senior to the other, who also wore dark green uniforms with silver buttons. They looked after the Rolls Royce and the station wagon. Mr Raphael did not keep any horses. He was not a riding man.

On the whole, the indoor and outdoor staff got on well together when they did meet, although the butler and housekeeper endeavoured to make it clear they regarded themselves as being a degree superior to all other members of staff, outdoor as well as in. Mr Grubb willingly conceded to the housekeeper her right to have her own way indoors, a right challenged only by the butler. But I noticed, on occasions, he did not hesitate to point out one fact to both of them. The whole of the outdoor area was Mr Grubb's domain. Something, which if he had a mind to, Mr Grubb could make crystal clear to any member of staff, indoor or out, whatever their position.

Mr Grubb was always ready to recite two things. First, the only orders Mr Grubb ever accepted were the ones given to him by Mr Raphael personally. Mr Grubb used to go up to the "big house" each morning to see Mr Raphael and get his instructions for the day. Secondly, as Head Gardener, Mr Grubb, and Mr Grubb alone, was responsible for passing on any orders or instructions to members of the outdoor staff.

As usual, the married workers had their own cottages, although not all of them were on the estate. Mr. Raphael owned quite a lot of property in Shenley village itself and in the countryside around it. But as a single man, I knew I would not be given one. I was expected to live in the "bothy", a cottage used as a communal home by the unmarried members of the outdoor staff. This was the usual arrangement on private country estates. The young men stayed in the "bothy" during the week but, if at all possible, left to go to their own family homes as soon as work was finished on Saturday. They returned on the Sunday night, sometimes having travelled quite a distance.

Fortunately, my home was less than a couple of miles away, so I used to go back there at weekends as often as I could. If you left the "bothy" during the week for any reason, even if you went back home because you were sick, you did not get a full week's pay. But if you were ill and still stayed in the "bothy", you got your pay as usual.

The "bothy" was about a quarter of a mile from the "big house", but linked to it by telephone. Mr Raphael took a close, personal interest in the progress of his plants in the greenhouses. He would often ring up to enquire how certain delicate specimens were getting along. And the "bothy" being right next to the greenhouses, whoever answered was able to nip out, take a look and tell him. The "bothy" was a good size. It had three rooms and a kitchen downstairs. The kitchen was particularly well-equipped with a generous supply of crockery and cooking utensils. Upstairs were three bedrooms, a toilet and a bathroom. All the bed linen was provided.

The foreman "flowers under glass" and foreman "fruit under glass" each had one of the smaller bedrooms to themselves, a privilege accorded them because of their status. The under-chauffeur slept in the smallest room downstairs, so small it was almost a cupboard. As well as taking a turn at driving the Rolls Royce and station wagon, he had an extra job of mowing all the lawns with the motor mower. I slept in the biggest bedroom with four of the other journeyman. Like them, I had my own bed and a very small chest of drawers. But I kept all my valuables and prized personal possessions securely stowed away in a large black trunk. This was tucked out of sight under my bed. I carried the key with me at all times. It was the usual practice for anyone living as I did. A local lad, about fourteen years old, acted as our "bothy boy". We paid him to cook our breakfast. It had to be ready to eat at eight o'clock sharp when we started our breakfast break. For the rest of the day he helped out in the greenhouses with the other young boys. A local woman came in daily. She made the beds, cleaned and cooked our midday lunch and evening meal. We took our personal washing home.

We had an ample supply of milk from the home farm. Our "bothy boy" collected it first thing every morning. It was only skimmed milk, but if you had to stay in the "bothy" over Christmas, you got full cream milk as a special treat. We also got a regular supply of fresh vegetables from the kitchen garden. But we had to buy the rest of our food ourselves.

We made sure every man contributed his share of the cost of the food. We had a special system. Each week, we added up the amount of money our daily woman had spent. Then the name of each man and the money he owed was chalked on a small blackboard. This was known as the "grub score". The "grub score" was put on display in the dining room and as each man paid what he owed, his name was crossed off the list. The foreman "flowers under glass" was the oldest and therefore the most senior, so he was responsible for collecting the money and erasing the names.

CHAPTER
NINE

I was to work as a journeyman under the foreman "fruit under glass". On my first day he gave me a small all-purpose knife. I had to buy anything else I needed myself. I even had to buy my own gardening apron, the working uniform I was supposed to wear all the time. I chose one made of very hardwearing navy blue cotton. It had a row of small pockets along the bottom. They proved very useful.

A few tools were provided for the men working on the "pleasure gardens". They included knives for pruning and disbudding and a pair of secateurs. These were not like the modern ones. They had no spring and were more like a pair of pincers. The tools the men were given hung on nails hammered into the wooden walls of a small tool house. The name of the man who used each particular set was scribbled above them in chalk. No member of staff, other than the man named, ever dared touch a single one of them.

Each morning, the housekeeper used to tell Mr Grubb what fruit and vegetables were required that day. Whether she discussed the order with Mrs Raphael first I have no idea. Mr Grubb himself, and only ever Mr Grubb, passed the housekeeper's order on to the gardening staff. We then loaded whatever produce had been requested into a large basket. It was kept especially for that purpose and for that one purpose alone. And Mr Grubb, and only ever Mr Grubb, carried the loaded basket up to the "big house" and handed it over to the housekeeper personally.

There were about fifty big greenhouses at Porters Park. One was crammed with camellias. They were planted in the ground and trained to grow up the sides of the greenhouse. A few contained melons, tomatoes and cucumbers. But most contained carnations, hundreds, hundreds and hundreds of carnations.

The gardening staff who grew the fruit and vegetables had one target to keep in mind at all times. Their job was to ensure that, throughout the year, whatever the weather or season, a supply of their produce was available for as long a period as possible for the residents of the "big house" and their guests.

For the foreman "fruit under glass" and his staff it meant, as far as was humanly possible, always having a constant supply of fresh fruit of some sort ready for picking, especially those varieties that could not be grown out of doors or could only be produced in the kitchen garden for a month or so when they were in season. For example, we had to have strawberries and peaches available as soon after Christmas as we could manage.

As the journeyman working under the foreman "fruit under glass", I helped him look after nine greenhouses. Four of them contained peach trees. Three of these were heated. One was not heated. The peach trees inside the four greenhouses had been carefully chosen. The fruit they produced ripened at different times. We had early fruiting varieties of peach trees such as "Early Rivers", which ripened particularly quickly. Some trees fruited half way through the season. Others were late fruiting varieties. Usually, we reckoned to begin the first picking of peaches very early in May, and to have the fruit available until late in the summer.

No space was wasted in the four greenhouses. Strawberry plants were grown in pots on long wooden shelves running the length of each peach house. The first fruit from these was usually ready early in March. Sometimes even before that. We relied on these plants to provide sufficient strawberries from then on until the outdoor crop in the kitchen garden was ready.

Two of the other greenhouses contained figs, plus a plentiful supply of hairy Cape Gooseberries, a very popular fruit at that time. Two varieties of figs were grown: the Black Turkey, which fruited early, and the Brown Turkey, which fruited later. Both were grown in pots. Mr Raphael was very partial to a fresh fig, so we tried to have one ready for him almost every morning of the year. I saw quite a lot of Mr Raphael as a matter of fact. He often used to wander round the greenhouses, personally checking on the progress of his fruit and flowers, especially his figs. But the rule was to speak only when spoken to. And it was strictly observed. You never ever spoke to him unless he spoke to you first.

The remaining three greenhouses in our care were all vineries. Again they housed early and late fruiting varieties. One was Muscat of Alexander, an early fruiting vine. It produced grapes of a delicate yellowy green colour, of excellent quality. Another called Lady Downes had sweet round black grapes. The fruit from a third, Black Homburg, was a deliciously juicy, black, oval shape. The roots of all the vines were outside the greenhouses. A generous layer of bone meal was always sprinkled over them just before they were due to flower.

Grapes were constantly being requested by the residents of the "big house", so we tried to make especially sure a supply was available for as long a period as possible. In order to manage this we grew a few very early flowering vines in pots in the vineries. We could cut bunches of grapes from these well before the fruit on the main vines was ready. Then, as soon as that fruit began to ripen we carefully inspected it. We were interested only in those bunches without a blemish of any kind. We used to cut these from the vine in such a way that generous portions of their supporting stalks remained attached. The stalks were then pushed into specially shaped glass bottles that contained water and a small piece of charcoal.

All the bottles were taken to a special storeroom. It was lined with wooden shelves which had a row of holes cut into them along their length, and we dropped the bottles into the holes. The bottles were too big to slip right through. But their special shape made them lean over to one side at an angle so the bunches of grapes lay in a horizontal position, supported by the wooden shelves, but their stalks were still in the water. In this way, the fruit remained succulent and fresh for quite a long time. And the water in the bottles did not need changing, because the pieces of charcoal kept it pure and clear.

Every bunch we stored in this way had to be regularly inspected. And we carefully cut out any grape that had "shanked", that is its skin had become dull and shrivelled. We used a pair of special grape scissors. These had extra long, thin, cutting blades so you could probe right into the centre of a bunch without damaging the fruit. The storeroom containing the grapes in bottles was always kept locked. Anyone wanting to go in it for any reason had to apply to Mr Grubb, in person, for the key.

Like the rest of the outdoor staff, I was expected to be up and on the job by six o'clock in the morning. I did a twelve-hour day, working until six in the evening all the year round, except for Saturdays when I finished at two. I had a break for my breakfast at eight o'clock. But I had to be back at work again by a quarter to nine. Then I had another break, from one until two, for my midday meal. Both meals were eaten at the "bothy". These two breaks were the only ones I had. And while I was working in the greenhouses, I was not allowed even the quickest of puffs at either a cigarette or pipe. Mr Grubb did not actually have to see a man smoking. His nose could detect the slightest whiff of tobacco smoke from either, hours after they had been put out. And his eyes were always on the alert for any tell-tale cigarette ends hurriedly pushed under a convenient upturned flowerpot.

I used to collect my pay on Friday afternoons at four o'clock. Whatever the weather, all the outdoor staff went to Mr Grubb's big detached cottage, a short distance from the "bothy", and lined up outside his office. Mr Grubb handed us our week's pay in cash. We never had to sign our names anywhere to show we had collected it. I received one pound a week, but six shillings was deducted from it as rent for my keep at the "bothy".

All the outdoor staff were employed on the clear understanding that just one week's notice, from either side, was all that was required to terminate a man's stay there. Any of us could be given a week's notice if our work was not up to a satisfactory standard. But, I was told, Mr Grubb always managed to write some sort of reference for a man, even if he had to sack him for some reason. Having no reference was an extremely serious handicap. It usually meant you were not able to get another job.

An ordinary working day for me was passed in one or other of the nine greenhouses in the care of the foreman "fruit under glass". My first priority was to keep a constant eye on the temperature inside the greenhouses. I had to remember always to close their doors behind me to prevent any unnecessary loss of heat, especially in winter, and not to forget to open and close their windows in warmer weather, to stop them overheating. Twice a day, once in the middle of the morning and again at three o'clock in the afternoon, I had to water and syringe, that is spray fine jets of water over all the grape vines, peach trees and fig trees. I did this all the year, except for a very short period in the winter. I used heavy brass syringes. They must have been rather special, because I never saw the same type in use anywhere else. There were also other smaller jobs that had to be done regularly.

For the remainder of my working time I was potting and pruning endless plants and fertilising early varieties of vines and peaches. I used the tip of a soft white rabbit's tail to transfer the pollen from one plant to another. Sometimes I had to tie it to the end of a long stick, so I could reach up high to all the blossom.

The "fruit under glass" staff were also responsible for the "stove" plants, as they were known, in the large conservatory attached to the "big house". So I had to water and syringe the aspidistras, palm trees and orange trees in there. These were all grown in large pots. Once I dared to pluck an orange, but regretted it the moment my teeth sank into the flesh. It tasted awful. The fruit was intended for decoration only and not for eating. I also had to keep a check on the small heated mushroom house. It had two deep shelves, rather like great big trays, positioned one above the other, running along its length. Both were spread with a layer of well-turned horse manure. I had to check the temperature of this regularly with a thermometer and when it was just right, put in the mushroom spawn. The two shelves were used alternately. One contained mushrooms for cutting, the other a fresh lot of spawn. We had to syringe the trays daily while the mushrooms were growing.

Although I managed to get home most weekends while I was working at Porters Park, when it was my turn to do either "heavy" or "light" duty I had to stay in the "bothy" instead. Only the journeymen had to take a turn at these. Foremen were excused. My turn came round about every four to six weeks.

"Light" duty meant I had to stay in the "bothy" over the weekend and keep an eye on the plants. Twice each day, I had to water and syringe all of them, in all the greenhouses, not just those in the care of the foreman, "fruit under glass", and open the windows of all the greenhouses, if it were hot.

"Heavy" duty was much more strenuous. It lasted seven full days, not just over the weekend, from the early hours of Saturday morning until late the following Friday night. It meant during that time, in addition to my normal week's work from Monday to late Saturday afternoon, I was also responsible for the greenhouse boilers. I was responsible for them twenty-four hours a day.

While I was on "heavy duty", I was not supposed to leave the estate at any time, for any reason whatsoever. If something happened and I simply had to get away, I had to try to persuade one of the other journeymen to cover for me. But the other man would expect to be paid for doing it in my place. And Mr Grubb would have to be told first and say whether he agreed with the proposed arrangement. If the weather turned warmer, the boilers were allowed to go out. But the man on "heavy" duty still had to stay close at hand, in case the weather suddenly turned cooler. If the temperature in any of the greenhouses dropped below sixty degrees Fahrenheit at any time, I had to re-light the boilers immediately.

There were three boilers, one very large, the other two slightly smaller. When doing "heavy" duty, I had to get up extra early in the morning to "clinker" them. That is, shake out all the ash that had accumulated during the night, then recharge them with coke. I used a set of giant "clinker" irons, over twelve feet long and very heavy. It took quite an effort to lift them and prod the fires into life. But shovelling in the coke was even more tiring. The three boilers devoured coke by the cartload. In winter they sometimes needed refuelling three times a day. Fresh supplies of coke were delivered almost daily. But "heavy" duty was not only tiring. It was dirty. The man on "heavy" duty always got priority in the bathroom on Friday nights.

After "clinkering" the boilers, I used to go back to the "bothy" to make a cup of tea for the men there. On the Sunday, I also walked to the home farm to collect our allocation of milk because our "bothy boy" did not come in on that day.

My week's "heavy" duty also meant that last thing at night I had to go round and securely lock every greenhouse. But even then I was still not finished. I had to get up three or four times in the night to check the temperature in all of them. We kept a special storm lantern in the "bothy" for the "heavy" duty man to use, so he could see his way round the greenhouses in the dark. If the temperature had fallen, I had either to re-light or to re-stoke the boilers, even if it were the middle of the night. And I still had to get up early next morning to "clinker" them and unlock all the greenhouses.

The flowers and produce in the greenhouses were worth a considerable amount of money. As Head Gardener, their care and safety was Mr Grubb's main responsibility. It was not unknown for Mr Grubb to appear among the greenhouses during the night, checking personally that the man on "heavy" duty was doing all that was expected of him. But Mr Grubb had the knack of being able to materialise anywhere on the estate, at any time, checking every member of the outdoor staff was doing the job he was being paid to do. And doing it in the right and proper way it should be done. If Mr Grub did happen to see any of us standing idle for a second, or even simply appear to be standing idle for a second, he immediately bawled out, at the top of his voice, his favourite instruction, "Get on with it".

Mr Grubb was, indeed, a strict disciplinarian, but he was also very fair. And he did have a genial side to him. While I worked at Porters Park, he never did or said anything, which gave me cause to dislike him. In fact, I seemed to get on well with him. I remember I had to do either "light" or "heavy" duty over Christmas and he carried a big Christmas dinner over to the "bothy" for me on a tray. I think the high standards maintained out of doors on the Porters Park estate owed a lot to the vigilant care and expert supervision of Mr Albert Grubb.

CHAPTER
TEN

Normally, members of the outdoor staff never set foot inside the "big house". We were not supposed to go near it. Even those workers whose gardening jobs might be expected to take them close to it at times always had to have a very good reason for being where they were. And, if inclined to linger there, a ready explanation for Mr Grubb as to why that particular job was taking so long.

However, because of the vast numbers of carnations grown in the greenhouses, I was often asked to help the foreman "flowers under glass". I did whatever he considered necessary, disbudding, staking, putting on collarettes. These were small open-ended circles of wire we clipped round the green base of the flower head, the calyx, to stop it from splitting. So the foreman sometimes took me with him when he went up to the "big house" to arrange the flowers. Surprisingly, this was always done by the outdoor staff, never by those indoors.

As with the fruit and vegetables, the housekeeper used to tell Mr Grubb, in the morning, what sort of flowers were needed. Mr Grubb then passed her instructions on to the foreman "flowers under glass".

The foreman "flowers under glass" always cut the flowers himself. I was not allowed to cut a single bloom, even if he had asked me to help him carry them up to the "big house" and arrange them. But Mr Grubb did not dare cut through a single flower stalk, either. This was a right reserved solely for the foreman "flowers under glass".

Arranging flowers in the "big house" was almost a daily occupation. Fresh ones were ordered for every dinner party. It was quite usual for these to be held as often as three or four times a week. Also guests were always being invited to stay for the weekend, especially when large shooting parties were organised. Fifteen or twenty people would regularly sit down to dinner. Many a time, there were even more.

There was a strict rule, which was always observed, when any of the outdoor staff went up to the "big house" to arrange the flowers. We only ever entered the "big house" in pairs. Apart from Mr Grubb, no member of the outdoor staff ever went in the 'big house" alone. I think it was because there were lots of small porcelain and silver items, vases, dishes, etc. lying about on small tables and window-ledges. Perhaps, it was thought, if we were by ourselves, we might feel tempted to slip one or two of them in our pocket. In fact, the "big house" was crammed with valuable pictures and large expensive ornaments. As a safety precaution, Mr Raphael employed a night watchman to patrol the grounds around it from dusk to sunrise.

The foreman "flowers under glass" and I carried the flowers up to the "big house" in a large shallow basket known as a "botch". We always went in through the back entrance, of course. And immediately took off our shoes and put on the slippers kept just inside the back door, especially for us to use, so there was no risk of our leaving dirt on the carpets. The housekeeper showed us up the back staircase and waited in each room until we had finished. Usually, we took about an hour to arrange the flowers in all the rooms. But it took longer if a dinner party were arranged.

We always started in the dining room on the first floor. Our freshly cut flowers were put in the vases on the mantelpiece above the fireplace and on the window-ledges. Then we removed any dead or dying blooms from the flowers we had taken out of the vases in the dining room and put these in the sitting room. We tidied the flowers we took from the sitting room and carried them through to the hall. Those already in the hall passed their final days of life in the servants' quarters. But if a dinner party had been arranged for that evening, the dining table had to be decorated as well. First, we carefully pinned a long length of smilax round the edge of the table. Smilax is a creeper with very dark green leaves. And very attractive it looked against the snowy white damask tablecloth. We grew the smilax in the greenhouses, training it to grow vertically up lengths of strong black cotton. That way, it was easy to measure and cut off exactly the right amount we needed. Sometimes, if it were an extra special party, we used to drape lengths of smilax between the vases of flowers on the dining table, from one rim to the next. It made the table look very pretty indeed.

We used five elegant crystal vases. The tallest one we put in the centre of the large oval table, the four smaller ones went in pairs either side. They were all filled with the same type of flowers. The varieties were never mixed. The flower usually requested for the dining room was the carnation. At that time carnations were expensive to grow. They needed a heated greenhouse and the care of a gardener who was a carnation expert. So they were looked on as a prestigious flower. In fact for some people, the carnation was the most prestigious flower of all. Many people considered them to be an emblem of the wealthy.

A special favourite was one of the malmaison strains of carnation. The malmaison strains of carnation were popular everywhere. I believe the first plant was developed from the strain of carnation known as the Remontant. That first plant happened to be the same colour as a new rose introduced soon after the death of the Empress Josephine. Her home was called Malmaison, so the new rose had been called "Souvenir de la Malmaison" and the new carnation was given the same name.

It was the custom to give men's names to those malmaisons having darker coloured flowers. King Arthur was a deep scarlet, The Colonel a cherry red. The plants producing paler blooms were given ladies' names. Duchess of Westminster was rose pink, Nell Gwynne a pure white.

However, Mr Raphael had totally lost his heart to just one particular malmaison carnation. It was known as Princess of Wales. It had only been recently developed but was already much sought after. Princess of Wales had an exceptionally fine salmon pink bloom and a lovely perfume. We were asked to display Princess of Wales on the dining table more often than any other carnation, especially when guests were invited.

Because of his love of carnations Mr Raphael was one of thirty Vice-Presidents of the Perpetual Flowering Carnation Society. The others included Prince Alexander Mesterchy of Russia, the Countess of Derby and Lord Rothschild. Mr Raphael's wife actually had a carnation named after her. The flower, Mrs C. F. Raphael, won an award of merit at one of their shows. Like many other owners of private country estates, Mr Raphael was also a member of the Royal Horticultural Society. He regularly exhibited his flowers, especially his malmaison carnations, in their shows in London and won several first prizes over the years.

I remember Mr Raphael sent four of the men, one being myself, up to a flower show in London. We stayed there for two or three days. All our expenses were met by him. Our job was to prepare and stake his flowers so they were ready for exhibition. Then we had to nurse them along for the duration of the show.

We had three wooden shelves on which to display our plants. They were positioned one behind the other but raised slightly above the one in front to form a tier. First, we draped a length of "bass" over them. "Bass" was a dark green, closely tufted material. It looked like grass and made an attractive background. Then we carefully positioned our pots on it. We had about sixty or seventy with us. All of them contained the Princess of Wales strain of malmaison carnation. It was impossible to count how many flowers the plants had in bloom between them. But they made a magnificent display. The judges came round to inspect them just before the show opened to the public. They awarded Mr Raphael a cup for the best malmaisons entered.

During the exhibition our most important task was to ensure every plant was given the exact amount of water it needed. Not too little, not too much. So, each morning, we would tap the side of every pot in turn using a small cane with a tiny metal tip on the end. If the pot sounded hollow we knew a little more water was needed.

Shortly after my visit to London, an incident occurred on the estate which could have had very serious consequences for me. It might even have led to my instant dismissal. Mr Raphael frequently wandered round the greenhouses, seeing for himself just how well his plants were faring. As I have already mentioned, he was very partial to having a fresh fig at breakfast time and one day, as it happened, an especially fine large Brown Turkey fig caught his eye. It promised to develop into a really splendid juicy specimen. Day after day, he came down to the greenhouse and gleefully noted how his fig was gradually getting riper and riper. Clearly, Mr Raphael was happily anticipating his enjoyment when he actually ate his appetising morsel. And he could see for himself, the day he would have that pleasure was getting closer and closer.

Then, one morning, I went into the greenhouse and was horrified. Mr Raphael's special fig was missing. It had vanished. There was not the slightest trace of it. Was I worried! None of the outdoor staff were supposed to touch any of the fruit, at any time, unless actually ordered to do so by either Mr Grubb or the foreman "fruit under glass". Of course, I had to go to Mr Grubb and tell him at once. He came back with me to the greenhouse and closely inspected the tree for himself. Such a disaster meant there was only one thing he could do. He had to go and report the mystery of the disappearing fig to Mr Raphael personally. He went up to the "big house" immediately. I stood and waited beside the stripped tree, convinced Mr Grubb suspected I was the culprit. I was sure he thought I was the only person who could possibly have stolen the fig. Not only stolen it but taken it and eaten it myself. And, of course, Mr Raphael would think the same thing, too. The chances were he might force me to leave his employment immediately or, at the very least, insist I had a week's notice.

An infuriated Mr Raphael was in such a rage he practically came hurtling through the greenhouse door. Right away, shouting at the top of his voice, he accused me, as the journeyman responsible for the fig tree, of taking his fig and eating it. Of course, I denied it at once. Then Mr Grubb, as ever, coolly determined to get to the bottom of things, asked me if I had seen anyone hanging around the greenhouses recently. At first, I said no. Then I remembered. I had seen someone. I told Mr Raphael I had seen his twelve-year-old daughter walking near the greenhouses the previous evening. His daughter had not gone away to a boarding school like her brother, she had lessons at home from a governess.

Mr Raphael sent for his daughter at once. When she came along to the greenhouse her father asked her about the missing fig. Totally unabashed, she admitted she was the one who had plucked her father's favourite fig off the tree and eaten it. Mr Raphael seemed even more enraged than before, on hearing it was his own daughter who had snatched his titbit and scoffed it. There and then, in front of Mr Grubb and myself, he put his daughter across his knee and gave her a real good spanking. Perhaps his action was, in part, intended as a sort of apology to Mr Grubb and myself, for having accused his staff of stealing.

As well as taking a great interest in his plants, Mr Raphael also took a great interest in his brother's racehorses. Mr Walter Raphael's horse, Louviers, had almost won the Derby a few years before. But the judges decided another horse, Minoru, had just beaten Louviers at the winning post. At the time, some people thought this was rather a controversial verdict.

While I was at Porters Park, Mr Walter Raphael entered another of his horses, a grey filly called Tagalie, in that year's Derby. She had been bred in France and had already won two small races there, when he bought her, although I believe he did not pay a lot for her. She was only a small horse and, apparently, had the reputation of not being very robust. She had never given any indication she was capable of winning a big classic race.

But the evening before the Derby, Mr Cecil Raphael, my employer, came down to the "bothy" as he often did, to chat to us about various things. He suggested we should all back his brother's horse. I took his advice and put a shilling on her. Tagalie led from the start and eventually won by four clear lengths. The odds had been good, so I picked up a welcome extra bit of money. At that time, Tagalie was only the fifth filly ever to win the Derby since it began, and only the second grey to do so. Some years later one of her great-great granddaughters won the Chilean Derby.

CHAPTER
ELEVEN

Occasionally I had one or two seasonal interruptions to my normal daily working routine. Sometimes I acted as a ball boy for Mr Raphael and his visitors, when they played tennis. I did this only if Mr Raphael's son was not available for some reason: when he was away at school for example. A ball boy was needed because Mr Raphael was rather rotund. As were most of his wealthy friends. So rotund, in fact, he and they had some difficulty bending down to pick up the balls lying on the ground.

I remember instead of netting, the two tennis courts had a beautiful, thick yew hedge round them. It was six feet tall and about two feet wide and always immaculately clipped. When the tennis finished I received two shillings as a tip for my efforts. I also enjoyed a very special privilege. I was allowed to go into the "big house" through the front door and sit in the butler's pantry, a sort of little cubbyhole, just off the main hall. The butler served me afternoon tea, bread and butter with jam and a slice of cake.

I was also excused my normal work for several days during the shooting season. I used to act as a beater with some of the other men. We went ahead of the guns, beating the undergrowth with a stick to flush out the pheasants. Often we passed through the very same woods where Stanley and I frequently trespassed as children, mischievously removing cartridges from the trip guns set up by the gamekeepers, to give them warning of poachers.

But for the staff as a whole, the most exciting event of the year occurred in January. That was when Mr Raphael held the annual servants' ball. All the estate workers and their wives were invited, but no girlfriends of the unmarried male staff were allowed to attend, or the boyfriends of unmarried female staff. Even so, there must have been between fifty to sixty people present. Several big tables were set up in the ballroom, because it was bigger than the dining room. I remember its beautiful, shiny, wooden floor and the lovely paintings hanging on the walls.

Caterers from outside prepared and served the meal, so the kitchen staff could go to the party, too. No individual place names were on the tables. The different groups of workers were each allocated a particular section. We knew there would be ample supplies of food. We had soup first, then turkey with all the trimmings and vegetables. Followed by Christmas pudding and mince pies, jelly and cream. Finally, we were served a generous supply of fresh fruit and nuts.

Mr Raphael always enjoyed the servants' ball. He and his wife, plus any of their guests who happened to be visiting them, acted as our waiters. Mr Raphael entered wholeheartedly into the spirit of the occasion. He always carefully draped a white table napkin over his arm before going round the tables to take our individual orders for drinks. There was complete freedom for everyone to choose whatever they wanted. In fact, wine, beer and spirits were available throughout the evening.

After the meal, everything was cleared away so we could dance to gramophone records. It was all done properly. Small cards with pencils attached were handed out to the ladies so their partners could write their names beside the dances printed on them. And there were lots of fun and games as well as the dancing. Mr Raphael joined in all that, too. But, at the first stroke of midnight all the fun ended. And it was back to the "bothy" for me.

I still had my leisure time to fill, but now I had some new diversions. The Porters Park estate had its own cricket team. The clubhouse and cricket pitch were provided and maintained by Mr Raphael, as was all the equipment, the bats and balls etc. The only thing the staff were expected to supply were their own "whites". Regular practice sessions took place most summer evenings, and at weekends as well, when we were not playing a match. Only people who worked on the estate could play in the cricket team. There was considerable competition for every place in it. Even the man on "heavy" duty was excused work, if he were chosen to play in a cricket match: the only time this ever happened. If my name was on the team list I did not go home that weekend. I was only an average batter. I got my place because I was a better bowler. Mr Grubb, at fifty, was too old to play in the team. But he always enjoyed a game of cricket with us and was still quite a useful bowler.

Usually, we played matches against local village teams — South Mimms, North Mimms, Radlett, Shenley and London Colney. But occasionally we played teams from other local private country estates. Although there were not too many of these because the smaller estates did not have a big enough staff to field a team regularly.

The staff on the Porters Park estate were also allowed to play golf on the estate golf course. But only when Mr Raphael and his guests were not using it, of course. We had to supply our own clubs, a problem usually solved by a newcomer buying the set of clubs owned by the member of staff he was replacing. But we could only use the rough patches of grass alongside the proper greens, in case we damaged the turf.

Meanwhile, I was continuing to visit my family most weekends and was still going regularly to village dances, usually to the ones held in Shenley. I remember on one particularly cold winter's day, it happened to be a Friday, I discovered my dancing shoes needed repairing. I decided to take them to the cobbler's shop in Radlett, a small village about one and a half miles from the estate's back entrance. By the time I was on my way back it had got dark. Then I met Agnes, one of the laundry maids, and we walked the rest of the way together. I had my carbide acetylene lamp with me and when we reached Porters Park, Agnes, being rather nervous, asked me to see her safely up to the "big house".

So I walked with her from the back entrance all the way up to the back door. Then, keeping a careful eye out for the patrolling night watchman, I headed for the "bothy". I decided the quickest route would be to take a short cut across the tennis courts. I did so safely and was strolling casually past the powerhouse, when I heard the last thing I wanted to hear at that particular moment. The voice of Mr Grubb. He was inside the powerhouse talking to one of the engineers. I did my best to creep away, as quietly and as quickly as I could. But the ever-alert Mr Grubb must have heard me, because he called out, asking who was there. Of course, I did not reply. I was not supposed to be anywhere near the "big house", even in the daytime. Certainly not at night, although it was not so very late in the evening. I was sure my acting as an escort for Agnes, because she was afraid of the dark, would not be accepted as a reasonable excuse for me being where I was.

My silence did not deter Mr Grubb. He called out his question even more loudly. I knew he must be certain someone was outside. Then he shouted very loudly indeed. I realised he knew someone was there. He was sure to come out and try to find whoever it was. My heart pounding, I raced the remaining short distance to the "bothy". But, having got there, I did not dare risk opening the door and going inside in case Mr Grubb heard me. Suddenly, I though of a good hiding place. Hurriedly, I dived into some thick laurel bushes, just behind the "bothy". Only then did I discover that, just like Cinderella, I had lost one of my dancing shoes. Mr Grubb arrived at the "bothy" and called to the men inside to come out. He told them an intruder was around and they were to help to catch him. In my desperation I crawled right into the centre of the group of laurels. But the dead leaves and twigs lying on the ground under them continually crackled and rustled as I moved. I knew this was certain to give me away, eventually. Then I had an idea. I picked up a large stone and threw it high in the air. It came down on the other side of the laurels. Loudly rattling through their branches as it fell. All the men began to rush over to that side of the bushes, creating a lot of noise as they went.

Now was my opportunity — any sounds I made would be covered by the louder noise the men were making. I crept out of the bushes on the opposite side to where the men were gathered. Then I walked round to where they were standing and calmly asked what was happening. I pretended to help them search for the intruder for some time. But what I was really looking for was my lost dancing shoe. Trust Mr Grubb. He was the one who found it. He even tested it for size against the trail of footprints I had left. A row of them was clearly marked in the frost covering the grass on the tennis courts. Of course, I did not dare claim the shoe as mine. So that escapade cost me the price of a new pair of dancing shoes.

CHAPTER
TWELVE

Every Friday, Mr Grubb used to bring a copy of *The Gardeners' Chronicle* over to the "bothy". I quite enjoyed looking at all the photographs of the "big houses" in it. Usually these were angled in such a way that the "big house" was seen set against some particularly attractive feature in its surrounding gardens. I could also read reports about gardening activities on other private country estates, such as how new varieties of plants were faring or details of an estate's success with one particular flower. Then there were helpful hints on the practical aspects of gardening, the best way to prune a certain type of shrub and how to eradicate pests in the greenhouse.

The newspaper also contained lists of vacancies for gardening staff on other country estates. A typical advertisement read something like this, "Wanted: experienced, energetic young man for Lawns and Pleasure Gardens. Bothy, milk and vegetables provided. Duty every fourth week". Sometimes it just said, "Take a turn with Duty", The duty referred to being, of course, "light" duty and "heavy" duty. Sometimes an advertisement indicated there was no bothy. But every one ended with the same phrase, "References required". In those days personal references were essential. You could not hope to get any sort of decent job without a good set of references. So you never left a post without getting one. And you looked after your references, very carefully. I have still got mine.

Men seeking gardening work also advertised in *The Gardeners' Chronicle*. They always said whether they were married or single. And, if married, how many children they had, their ages and, sometimes, whether boys or girls. Occasionally, an employer would insert a courteous notice, thanking all who had replied to their recent advertisement but indicating the post had now been filled. A small section was headed, "Appointments". Anyone getting a job as Head Gardener or Bailiff on one of the bigger private country estates merited a mention in it. A short paragraph would give his name, the date of his appointment and details of his working career to date.

A year or so before I went to work at Porters Park, a report appeared in *The Gardeners' Chronicle* about the estate. Under the heading, "Early flowers of Malmaison carnation", it said, "At a meeting of the Royal Horticultural Society on February 16th, much interest was evinced in a group of Souvenir de la Malmaison carnations, shown by C. F. Raphael, Esq., Porters Park, Shenley, Herts. (gr. Mr Grubb)". The article went on to say, "Mr Grubb is very successful in the culture of this type of carnation and has had a display of flowers, which was greatly admired, by visitors to the garden. The following remarks by Mr Grubb on various agricultural details will, therefore, be read with interest".

Mr Grubb then passed on to the readers of the newspaper some advice based on his own long horticultural experience as it related to the growing of malmaison carnations. "Manure should be applied freely until the buds show colour, but at that stage it should be discontinued altogether. The manure I use most is Bentley's carnation manure and, for a change, manure water obtained from the soaking of sheep's droppings, gathered in the summer time, under trees in the park, where the sheep go for shade. The malmaisons are greatly benefited by this latter cheap manure". Mr Grubb also advised, "syringing them (the malmaisons) occasionally with 'Carvita' so the plants remain free from rust and disease. After this, the grower may venture to keep the plants a little warmer, but it is important at all times of the year, to give them plenty of ventilation and the cooler the plants are kept when resting the better." Mr Grubb named some of the malmaison carnations being grown at Porters Park. "Maggie Hodgson is one of the finest malmaisons. Duchess of Westminster is indispensable, being an early variety and one that will thrive anywhere. But the Princess of Wales is the variety most grown here, it having one of the largest flowers."

But misfortune could strike even the best-run private country estate's gardens. A short time later, a representative of *The Gardeners' Chronicle* called on Mr Raphael again. The reason was that, "On many occasions, excellent groups (of flowers) have been

94

exhibited from Porters Park, very early in the season. A large contribution was to have been made to the Holland Park show, so I visited Porters Park especially to see those plants." But the caller discovered gardening life there had not been going quite as the Head Gardener had planned, for he reported, "I found Mr Grubb almost in tears for, owing to the dull weather, the blooms had not fully developed, therefore the idea of exhibiting them at Holland Park was abandoned and instead they will be shown at the Vincent Hall a fortnight later."

The report on his visit to Porters Park continued, "I noticed two hundred plants of Princess of Wales in eight inch pots, with eight or nine flowers to a plant. The Colonel, a fine new variety, with flowers nearly six inches in diameter, was at its best. King Arthur, Lady Rose and King Oscar were especially fine. The collection included seven hundred plants in eight-inch pots and one thousand plants in six-inch pots. Tree carnations for winter flowering are grown in equal numbers."

Happily, a few issues later, better news was recorded in the columns of the newspaper, "The excellent group of carnations shown by C. F. Raphael, Porters Park, Shenley (gr. Mr Grubb) at Vincent Hall was comprised of varieties of the Souvenir de la Malmaison type. It was an extensive and boldly arranged group, a number of large Nephrolepis Ferns being disposed at intervals and affording a pleasing relief to the flowers. Many of the carnations were of the Princess of Wales variety, those being shown were large, well-flowered plants, the individual blooms being remarkably fine." The report noted the Floral Committee awarded Mr Raphael a gold medal for the display. The first prize for that class of flower.

I fully endorse Mr Grubb's comments in the earlier report about the beneficial effects of using manure made from sheep's droppings. I used to gather them up in a bucket. Fill it with water. Stir the contents well and leave them to soak for two or three days. Then I drained off all the liquid. I used it about once a week on carnations, diluted, if necessary. I have also found it gave excellent results with tomatoes.

Although I was very happy at Porters Park, there were my hopes for the future to consider. I knew I had to move on. And keep on moving. I needed to work on different types of estates. That was the only way I could get enough experience backed up by the essential fistful of written references which would confirm I was fully qualified for a position of either Head Gardener or Bailiff. I knew it was time for me to keep an eye on the jobs being offered on other private country estates.

Mr Grubb knew I wanted to leave and the reason why. Decent old boy that he was, he brought *The Gardeners' Chronicle* over to the "bothy" one Friday and pointed out a job advertised in it. He thought it might suit me. I thought so, too. I was delighted. It offered me promotion. It was for a foreman. If I got it, I would already have taken one step up the private country estate employment ladder.

Mr Grubb knew the Head Gardener concerned, a Mr McIntyre. Most Head Gardeners seemed to know each other. Mr Grubb offered to speak to him on the phone. And he did so. Telling me afterwards the job was mine, subject to a satisfactory personal interview with Mr McIntyre, himself. As Head Gardener, Mr McIntyre had the right to appoint his own staff, so his opinion would be the only one that mattered. I saw him and got the job.

But I was careful not to leave Porters Park without a reference. Mr Grubb wrote me a nice one. It reads, "This is to certify, that Jack Sears was employed in these gardens, for about two and a half years. He is very willing and obliging, smart and intelligent and a good worker and I shall at all times, be pleased to recommend him. Sgd. A. Grubb".

On my last day at Porters Park, when Mr Grubb came over to the "bothy" to say goodbye, he asked me a question, saying it had been on his mind for some time. Ever since the night he had found a dancing shoe, in fact. He wondered whether I was the person he had heard moving about the grounds that night. I had to admit that, indeed, it was me. Then, Mr Grubb put his hand in his pocket, pulled out half a sovereign and pressed it into one of mine, commenting quietly,

"You're the only bugger who's ever caught me out."

CHAPTER
THIRTEEN

I had got my first promotion. I was now foreman "fruit under glass". My new position was on a private country estate, not so very far away, at Stanmore about five or six miles from Shenley. The Warren House estate, as it was called, was even bigger than Porters Park. It spread to so many acres I could not even begin to count them. I understood from the staff already working there when I arrived, that the owner was a Baroness Bischoffsheim, an elderly lady and a widow. I only ever saw her once and then from a distance. The Baroness was well-known for her interest in orchids. Quite a few were grown from seed, a difficult task. But, like most owners of private country estates, she was also very keen on growing carnations.

I found working conditions at Warren House very different from those at Porters Park. All the greenhouses at Porters Park had been grouped together, in one place. So I used to see quite a few of the other outdoor staff at some time during the day. But on the Warren House estate everything was spread out over a far wider area. For example, the kitchen garden was quite close to the "big house", but the greenhouses were not. So I only got to know those members of the outdoor staff who actually worked alongside me, plus the few who lived with me in the "bothy".

But I found out Mr McIntyre had about six men working on the eighteen-hole golf course. While the foreman "pleasure gardens" had three journeymen to help him, the foreman "flowers under glass" worked with four journeymen. Three of them looked after four big greenhouses. Two others were full of carnations. The fourth journeyman was a carnation expert and he looked after those. The journeymen working for the foreman "flowers under glass" also looked after the plants in the large conservatory. This was close to the "big house" but not attached to it. How many journeymen, the foreman "kitchen garden" had I never knew. As it happened, I only stayed there for a short time and during that time I never met any engineers or carpenters, but I think some must have been employed somewhere on the estate.

As foreman "fruit under glass", I had full responsibility for seeing a constant supply of fruit was available for most of the year. I had two young lads to help me look after ten big greenhouses. In some of them I had fig trees in pots, lemon trees in pots and orange trees in pots. In amongst them were strawberries and Cape Gooseberries. Other greenhouses contained peaches, nectarines and a tremendous variety of pears. Five of the greenhouses were vineries. Some of the smaller vines produced only a few bunches of grapes a year. But these were particularly useful because they ripened very early in the year, in March, well before the main crop was ready.

Mr McIntyre used to come round every morning with the order for fruit for the "big house". Like Mr Grubb, he always took it up there himself. No-one else ever did. Like Porters Park, too, none of the outdoor staff were supposed to go near the "big house". So I have no idea how many indoor staff there were. But I know the Baroness employed an Austrian chef and not an ordinary English cook because, sometimes, he came down to the greenhouse and chose the fruit himself. Never picked it himself, of course. Only me, as foreman "fruit under glass", could touch it. Once, when the Baroness was away, the butler invited me to step through the front door of the "big house" into the entrance hall. I remember a magnificent open staircase lead up to the first floor. And growing beside it was a splendid palm tree in a pot. It must have been at least twenty-five feet tall.

I could see lots of big cars coming and going to and from the "big house" all the time, so the Baroness was doing a lot of entertaining. But the foreman "flowers under glass" must have collected all the flowers needed. Perhaps the indoor staff arranged them because I was never asked to help decorate either the dining room or any other room in it. Apart from supplying all the produce required, the daily routine of the outdoor staff did not appear to be affected in any way by the number of guests being entertained up at the "big house".

Once again, I lived in the "bothy" on the estate. It was a semi-detached cottage, the other half of the pair being the home of the Head Gardener, Mr McIntyre. But this "bothy" in no way offered the same standard of accommodation as the one at Porters Park. To begin with it was much older. What was more, judging by the gullies running the length of the ground floor, it had originally been a cowshed or some similar type of building. The kitchen was very poorly equipped, with very little crockery and very few cooking utensils. And there was no proper bathroom, only a shower.

Living with me in the "bothy" were two young lads who worked on the estate and two journeymen. One helped to look after the golf course. The other journeyman was the carnation expert. The "bothy" was run on exactly the same system as the one at Porters Park. We were supplied with milk and vegetables. A local woman came in daily, during the week, to do the cooking and cleaning. We had a "bothy boy" to get our breakfast.

The carnation expert was responsible for keeping the "grub score". He was also a professional boxer. He fought under the name of "Young Warner". Those of us living in the "bothy" spent a lot of our spare time helping him to keep fit. Many an occasion I squared up to him in a practice bout. Had it been a real fight, I would not have stood a chance. He used to go out running round the lanes and we would ride alongside him on our bikes, making sure he did not slacken off the pace. He did a lot of skipping during his training sessions. The rest of us used to count the number of times the rope went under his feet, continually yelling encouragement to keep him going just that little bit longer, the din getting louder and louder the longer he skipped. Until Mr McIntyre knocked loudly on the dividing wall as a signal he had had enough and thought it was time we quietened down.

On Sunday mornings we used to go rabbiting in the woods on the estate. A journeyman, who worked in the "pleasure gardens", had a dog and ferrets. The dog was only a mongrel, but an excellent rabbiter. He would eagerly sniff out the scent around the rabbit holes. Sometimes he even went down them. But, usually, it was the ferrets that flushed out the rabbits. These were caught as they tried to escape in nets spread over the other entrances to their warren. They were stunned with a thick stick and then their necks were broken. Back at the "bothy" we skinned and gutted them and they were ready for our housekeeper to make into a tasty stew.

My pay was now one pound and five shillings per week, less a small sum deducted as rent for the "bothy". My hours of work were the same as those at Porters Park. I used to get very thirsty in the warm greenhouses but, fortunately, I was able to come to a special little arrangement with the cowman. He brought me a glass of milk, cool and refreshing, every afternoon. In return, I gave him an occasional bunch of grapes or one or two small peaches. I was, after all, foreman "fruit under glass". Even so, I still had to take a turn with "heavy" and "light" duty. But, here, the man on "heavy" duty was allowed to go out in the evenings. In this, and in many other small ways, it seemed to me that the Warren House estate was not run with quite the same overall tight standard of discipline that Mr Grubb maintained at Porters Park.

I never heard any mention of a Christmas ball for the staff while I was there. And there was no cricket pitch, so no cricket team. But the staff were allowed to play golf on the golf course. Unfortunately, I had left my clubs behind at Porters Park, but I was able to buy another set from the carnation expert. I did not go to any dances. None seemed to be held locally.

I stayed less than a year on the Warren House estate. Just as I arrived the First World War started. The men in the big cars driving up to the "big house" began to wear all different types of military uniform, I noticed. Every one of them was smothered in gold braid. I heard that many of the men working on other local private country estates had already enlisted or were thinking of enlisting. But the war seemed very far away to me. I was preoccupied with other thoughts — how I could best equip myself with the right experience which would propel me to the top of the private country estate employment ladder.

Then I spotted an advertisement in *The Gardeners' Chronicle*. A foreman was needed at a small private boarding school for girls in Bushey, about four miles away. I was not particularly happy where I was so a move would be welcome. But what really tempted me, apart from the additional experience I would get, was the two pounds a week pay, a far higher than normal wage. The reason for this was the men were going off to war. They were beginning to be in short supply. So employers were having to offer higher pay to persuade those who remained to work for them.

I applied and got the job. I was especially pleased because it meant I would be working in my home county of Hertfordshire once more. Of course, I asked Mr McIntyre for a reference before leaving. He wrote, "Jack Sears was in the gardens here for about nine months, during which time he gave good satisfaction. I always found him sober and obliging. Sgd. Bill McIntyre. Head Gardener, Baroness Bischoffsheim".

Baroness Bischoffsheim died about eight years after I left the Warren House estate. She was then eighty-five. According to her obituary in *The Times*, she was born Clarisse Biedermann, one of seven daughters of the Court jeweller in Vienna. She married a Louis Bischoffsheim, a very wealthy man, whose family owned a bank in London. Prince Edward and members of the diplomatic corps regularly attended her parties, both those held at Warren House and at her London home, Bute House in South Audley Street. When the Baroness and her husband celebrated their golden wedding, they distributed one hundred thousand pounds between various charities.

I soon settled into my new job at the school even though the grounds were very small when compared with the estates which I had worked on previously. There were only about five acres in all with just four outdoor staff, a Head Gardener, a foreman who was me, plus two junior boys. One of the junior boys helped out in the greenhouses. The other spent his time in the kitchen garden. Another boy came in occasionally to look after the flowerbeds. There were only six greenhouses. I looked after them all. Some were for fruit, some for flowers. A lot of begonias were grown in pots for display inside the school. I remember I had a pet toad. He used to hang about the greenhouses, hopping in and out of them, his way of begging for worms. Again I lived in the small cottage which served as the "bothy".

But I stayed at the school for only a short time, just about nine months, in fact. It happened like this. Watford was my nearest big town and I used to go there occasionally at weekends. One Saturday afternoon I was walking along Watford High Street when I was stopped by a sergeant wearing the uniform of the Hertfordshire Yeomanry. I knew what he wanted. The army needed more and more men. There were posters everywhere trying to persuade us to enlist. In those days no-one called at your home or place of work and hustled you off. Neither did you get a letter saying it was your turn to leave home and join the forces. You had to choose to go. You had to volunteer. But I had been so preoccupied with my own plans I had never seriously considered it.

The sergeant told me he was just back from fighting in France and was acting as a recruiting officer. He said my country needed me. It needed me now. I should be out there, fighting shoulder to shoulder with our boys on the front line. Spellbound by the glittering row of medals spread across his chest, I was quickly convinced. Awash with my newly aroused patriotism, I abandoned all thoughts of self-interest. My dream of one day becoming either a Bailiff or Head Gardener on a big private country estate, perhaps even one the size of Porters Park or Warren House, could wait. I had really big ideas about my future by this time. After all, I had already extended my working experience and gained promotion to foreman. I had nothing to lose. I could go off and fight the war, then, when it was all over, come back and resume my onward and upward career. At the time, I thought nothing in the world would happen that could possibly prevent it.

The sergeant gave me a free travel pass. This would get me to Hertford the following Monday for a medical examination. I returned to the school and told the Head Gardener I was about to enlist. He said I was being ridiculous. But I went to Hertford Town Hall the following Monday, passed my medical and was offered the King's shilling, the usual custom. My acceptance of it signalled my willingness to fight for my country. I was almost twenty-two, I had exchanged my gardener's apron for a soldier's uniform and was about to go to war.

Not a shred of fear drifted across my mind. I gave not a thought to the idea of there being the risk of personal danger to myself. Or even worse. I had only one strong feeling, that of excitement. I believed I had launched myself on the adventure of a lifetime.

CHAPTER
FOURTEEN

I had to report to the army depot in Hertford. There I was kitted out in peaked cap, khaki jacket, breeches and puttees, strips of material worn round the bottom of my trousers drawing them into my ankles. Then I was assigned to my regiment, the Hertfordshire Yeomanry. I started my basic training immediately. And very basic it was, too. There was a steep hill just outside the town. I had to run up it. Then when I got to the top, turn round and run back down again. Up again. Down again. Up again. Down again. I did this for most of the day, in full kit. The rest of the time I had bayonet practice. We used long wooden poles instead of the real thing. We had to keep jab, jab, jabbing away with them at sacks stuffed with straw. But this preliminary initiation did not last very long. At the end of the second week, I was transferred to Huntingdon and found myself one of twenty men forming a platoon. I was to receive a further session of training intended to turn me into a cavalryman. Regimental Sergeant Major Mills took charge of us. A proper terror he was, too. A real bugbear. Always screaming away at us at the top of his voice. He never tired of telling us what a rough lot we were. His job was to teach us exactly how to handle our horses. How to groom them. How to saddle them. And, most important of all, how to ride them out on parade. Of course, I had grown up with horses. But the other men tipped me off. They warned me on no account should I ever admit this. So, I tried hard not to give myself away.

But one morning, we took our horses out on parade and stood them in a long line, side by side, as usual. Sergeant Major Mills came walking along the line in front of us. Then suddenly, he stopped directly in front of my mount, and challenged me personally as to whether or not I already knew how to ride a horse. Obviously, the observant Sergeant Major must have detected I was more skilful than the others. Of course, I had to say yes. In that case, he pronounced, in future mine would always be the leading horse when we came out on parade. My heart sank. Fortunately, I did not have this responsibility for long because I was transferred again. I was sent to Tidmouth in Wiltshire, where I found myself a member of the Royal Scots Greys.

At this point, my parents applied for me to be given a week's "agricultural" leave. Food was getting scarce. Most of the men were away fighting the war now. Very few were left to cultivate the crops. So "agricultural" leave was granted to those soldiers who would spend the time working on the land. I had heard from my father how the nuns had asked him to plough up the "pleasure gardens" and part of the enormous lawn at the back of All Saints Convent to try and grow more food for themselves. It meant a greatly increased workload for him with almost no additional male help available. And this was happening just at the time my father's normal robust health had begun to fail him. In fact, my father's physical state was giving us all cause for concern. He was now a sick man. He was ill, so ill that he had been forced to give up his job as Bailiff at the All Saints Convent.

My father, my mother and my youngest brother, William, were no longer in their cottage on the All Saints estate. That went with the job of Bailiff. They had moved to Essex. They were living in a small rural village called Kelvedon Hatch, about three to four miles north of Brentwood, a small town eighteen miles east of London. My parents had seen an advertisement in a newspaper for a small house available to rent cheaply, together with five acres of land. They had driven over in their pony and trap, liked the place and decided to move there.

Although my father never said, I think I know why he made the move he did. He was a very proud man. For years he had lived in an area where he was well known and highly respected. He did not want the people who had known him there to become aware of the seriousness of his illness. But most of all he could not bear the people who had only known him as a successful man to see him and his family living in such altered circumstances.

The place my parents had decided to rent needed to be generally tidied and put in order. I was the only one who could do that. My father was too ill and William too young. Stanley had enlisted the day after me. We had done our basic training together at Hertford, but he had been sent overseas straightaway. Alice was now married and living with her husband in St Albans.

The railway voucher the army gave me got me as far as Brentwood. But I had to ask for further directions when I arrived at the station there. Three and a half miles north I was told. And the only way to get to Kelvedon Hatch was to walk. However, unbeknown to me, my mother had asked a friend, Mr Pinnock, landlord of The Eagle public house in Kelvedon Hatch, to meet me with his pony and trap. I must have covered close on two miles before I met him. He saw me trudging along in my uniform, carrying a heavy kit bag, and knew who I was at once. Although of course, I did not know him.

Mushroom Hall, where my parents were living, looked just like the first part of its name. It was a small, round, wooden, single-storey building. Its pointed thatched roof extended well beyond its outside walls to cover an encircling veranda. It did, indeed, look exactly like a giant mushroom. But it was no palatial Hall. Inside were just three bedrooms, a kitchen, a dining room and a drawing room. There was no bathroom. Just a primitive outdoor toilet, similar to the one we had before. My parents' only assets were a few cows, one or two pigs and some hens. Local people called in and bought the milk and eggs these produced. The few coppers they handed over were my parents' only source of income. My father had no pension and had already dipped deep into his savings.

110

I worked hard. Did all I could to help. I cut the grass. Trimmed hedges. Cleared ditches. Collected the eggs. Milked the cows. Cut the hay. Did general repairs around the house. But, at the end of the week, I had to go back to Tidmouth and leave my parents to cope at Mushroom Hall as best they could.

Almost immediately I returned, my cavalry unit was disbanded and I found myself back in the infantry. This time as a member of a West Yorkshire regiment. Apparently, this had suffered heavy losses in recent fighting and was now very short of men. But, almost at once, I was transferred yet again, to the Lancashire Fusiliers. It seemed they had suffered even heavier casualties than the West Yorkshire regiment. I received a further very brief spell of training, then I heard the Lancashire Fusiliers were off to France. By this time I was quite looking forward to seeing some action.

Early one morning, we crossed the English Channel and landed at Calais. We marched to a camp on top of a hill just outside the town where we were given breakfast. We got "bully beef", that is corned beef, with dry biscuits. Having travelled overnight we were allowed to rest for twenty-four hours. The following morning, at eight o'clock, we boarded some small buses. A soldier acting as our guide told us we were heading for the back of the front line. It was a place known as "Dicky Bush" camp, where we had some more food. While I was there, I spotted my first barrage balloon. I remember thinking the fighting could not be so very far away. I felt even more excited. Next, we marched about ten kilometres to Ypres and made camp for the night in an old brewery.

The following morning we got into wagons that ran on tracks and set off. We were heading straight for the front of the front line. When the wagons stopped, we got out. In single file, and in total silence, we walked hesitantly along slippery duckboard tracks. Totally awed by the surrounding ocean of mud and countless huge shell holes, gaping at us on either side. We could hear gunfire now. It was gradually getting louder and louder. I felt my spine beginning to tense. Each step I took was taking me nearer and nearer the fighting.

At one point, we had to step aside, off the duckboards, to let the Australian troops we were replacing pass through. They were in a dreadful, dirty state, smothered in mud from head to toe. While we were standing beside the duckboard tracks, a twelve-pounder gun suddenly opened up. It sounded so loud, it might have been right next to us. I almost leapt out of my skin. In fact, I was so startled my feet actually did do a little jump backwards, right into a deep shell hole filled to the brim with mud and water. Fortunately, a pal of mine quickly pushed his rifle butt towards me and hauled me out. I was now in the same state as the Australians. We walked on and managed to reach the front trenches safely and were delighted to find they had left behind some bread and jam for us.

I spent the next seven days and seven nights in the trenches. All the supplies we needed were brought in by mules. At the end of the seven days, we crept back along the duckboard tracks to the support lines. We stayed there for the next seven days and seven nights. That was the system. Seven days and nights in the trenches. Seven days and nights resting in the support lines. Backing up the support lines were the reserves. Sometimes, when we tried to walk back to the support lines, the duckboards were missing. Then we had to follow the tracks the mules had left in the mud, hoping they would lead us to where we were supposed to be heading. I was very fortunate at this time. I could hear the constant bombardment going on, but did not actually get involved in any heavy fighting, although once a stray piece of shrapnel caught me on the arm and inflicted a minor wound.

One incident I remember vividly. We were in the trenches and badly needed water. The only container we had was an empty petrol can. I was the person chosen to take this, creep out of the trench and search for a shell hole, one in which rainwater had collected. I quickly found what I needed. The only problem was the dead German soldier lying, almost submerged, in it. Suddenly, crouching down beside the hole, looking at him, I thought of all the souvenirs the other soldiers had collected, German badges and watches and other personal things. I fancied having some small souvenir myself, such as this dead soldier's watch. Reaching out, I managed to loop my fingers under the waistband of his trousers and began to pull him towards me. But his body was so decomposed, it fell apart as I touched him. Pieces of his flesh were actually stuck to his belt. I left him alone. I just filled my petrol can with the water he was lying in and ran back to my trench. It was not safe to stray too far looking for another more palatable shell hole.

After fighting in France for some weeks, my unit was suddenly transferred. Relief troops were urgently required in Belgium. Behind the front line there, I found some of the best dugouts I had ever seen. They were equipped with small huts with electric light laid on. But I enjoyed these comforts for only two days. Then I was on the move again. I remember the weather was very cold and snow lay on the ground the morning we were told we were off to the front line. Just that. We were given no further details. I was asked if I were carrying anything which might be of value to the enemy, should it happen to fall into his hands. By this time I knew they meant if I were killed or taken prisoner. I was told to put all my private papers, official documents and personal letters in a special large green envelope as these could provide the enemy with some clue as to my regiment. The green envelope was then taken away and I was ordered to take up my position. I knew now I was about to find myself in the war for real.

The fighting I experienced during the next few days was heavier than anything I had seen before. By this time I had been promoted to lance corporal and one morning I was ordered to take two men and check on an outpost some distance away. This particular outpost had changed hands several times. So, when no English sentry challenged us, we waited for a little while, then rushed inside. No-one was there, but we found German helmets and German stick bombs. Immediately, we retreated to our main trench. Our sergeant asked us why we were back so early, ahead of the time we had been told to return. We explained what we had found, but he told us we had disobeyed our instructions and placed us under arrest. Then he sent out another patrol to check on the outpost, again. They did not return until the next morning to report they had not even been able to find it. So we were released.

A few days later, I was told to go with eleven men, "squaddies", and take up a position in another isolated observation post, said to be about a quarter of a mile away from the German trenches. We set off in pouring rain and reached the observation post safely. Our orders were to stay there for the rest of the day and the following night. But at three o'clock in the morning the German guns suddenly opened fire. It was by far the heaviest bombardment I had experienced. The noise was indescribable. Incredibly loud. It seemed as if shells by the hundred were raining down and exploding all around us. I have no idea how or why we survived it.

As daylight came the bombardment lessened slightly, although it was still extremely heavy. Remembering what had happened to me a few days before, I told my men it was essential we should follow our instructions. We must attempt to rejoin our own front line. But I soon discovered this was going to be no easy matter. Shells were still falling and there was one of the thickest fogs I have ever experienced. But, worst of all, most of the trenches had caved in under the weight of the heavy shelling. Just a few short stretches were left, here and there, to provide us with shelter. Cautiously, we began to work our way back. Slowly we crept along, bent almost double at times, stopping to take cover in every length of trench we spotted. I was certain somewhere in the surrounding fog and mist German soldiers were on the move.

At this point, I lost one of my best mates. He would keep putting his head up above the top of the trench we were hiding in. He said he wanted to see if he could actually spot any "Jerries". I kept warning him to keep his head down, like the rest of us. But he took no notice. He lifted his head out of the trench one more time. Then, without making a sound, he dropped backwards into it. I saw a spurt of blood, beginning to ooze from a small hole in the middle of his forehead. We had to leave him where he fell.

Slowly, we moved on again, passing by and weaving in and out of what seemed to be hundreds and hundreds of dead and dying soldiers, strewn all over the ground. Some were moaning in agony. Others raised their hands to us for help. But there was nothing we could do for them. We had no medical supplies with us. We were handicapped by the fog. A handful of shells continued to fall, so we were still under fire. But, above all, we had our orders. We must get back to our unit. That had to be our first priority.

Then, creeping cautiously along, we came up against a further hazard. Suddenly I felt my eyes begin to sting. They quickly became so sore that tears rapidly gathered in them. At the same time, I started to cough and gasp. I found I could not breathe properly. I knew what it meant. Gas. Phosgene gas, I think they called it. Right away, we had to stop and put on our gas masks for a

116

time. It was difficult enough to see through them, even without the fog. Fortunately, the guns were firing fewer and fewer shells now, so conditions were a shade less difficult.

At last, we came across a German pillbox. I recognized it as one we had captured a day or so ago, before we had set out to man the observation post. Edging past, we crossed over the adjacent road and were safely behind the English front line once more. Silently I mouthed a prayer of thankfulness. We were safe. Or so I thought. But the position along the front line was very fluid at that time. Both sides were continually advancing and retreating, almost every day. They might surge ahead at one point and be held back at another. So the front line was not a line at all. It was a series of bulges. An attacking group of soldiers might succeed in breaking through and advancing well beyond their opposing side's front line, while just a short distance away, that same opposing front line refused to give any ground. That is what must have happened on this occasion.

Suddenly a stick bomb was thrown at us. It almost landed at my feet. The pillbox had been recaptured and reoccupied by German soldiers. Immediately, we all fell flat on our faces. After a few seconds, I risked cautiously raising my head. A German soldier was actually coming out of the pillbox. I took a shot at him but could not be certain whether I hit him or not. He either ducked or fell.

Quickly, we picked ourselves up and ran away through the mist, still hoping somehow, somewhere, to link up with our own troops. Spying a length of trench, we all dived in and began to creep along it as quietly as we could. Suddenly, hearing voices we looked up. Dozens of German soldiers were materialising along the trench's top edges. We were surrounded and totally outnumbered. There was only one thing we could do. And we did it. Hurriedly climbing out of the trench, we threw down our rifles and stood with our hands in the air. But even though we surrendered so promptly, the Germans still shot two of my men. Perhaps they intended this to be a warning to the rest of us, to behave ourselves or else.

As well as ourselves, the Germans had come across boxes of ammunition and supplies, abandoned in what was left of the trench. They seemed particularly cock-a-hoop at finding English cheeses amongst them. Taking advantage of the fact the bombardment had finally stopped, they made us carry everything to the back of their front line. Hauling my load along, I still did not fully realise that, from now on, I would be living a different kind of life. I was no longer a soldier, I was a prisoner of war.

CHAPTER
FIFTEEN

When we got to the back of the German lines, I had to join the other prisoners of war. They were standing in a long line. I was told to get to the back of it. It seemed to go on forever. There must have been thousands and thousands of us. We were ordered to start marching and had to walk for about ten kilometres. Then we were put into huge barbed wire cages. We were all very hungry but we got no food, just buckets of cold water, so we could have a drink. Next morning, we were lined up in a long column again, ready to set off. But first, our German guards walked along it and made us hand over our watches, rings, penknives, anything at all they fancied. I suppose they wanted their little souvenirs, too.

Then we began to march again. After we had been walking a little while an English aeroplane appeared. It swooped down low and the pilot "waved" its wings at us in salute. That cheered me up a little, but only a little. I still had not been given any food. I had not eaten a crumb for over twenty-four hours. Some of the others had gone almost two days without eating. We were all starving. Our extreme hunger provoked a crisis. The line marched past a field of turnips. I saw the turnips. So did my fellow prisoners of war. We all had the same idea. Simultaneously, every single one of us broke ranks and stampeded into the field. Frantically, we dug and stabbed our fingers into the black soil, prepared to risk being shot by the guards for the chance of gouging out one of the precious vegetables. The guards had to fire their guns in the air to get us back into line. Then, with everyone gnawing away at the uncooked, earth-stained turnips, we were on the march again.

Our column reached a town that had a railway station and we were loaded into cattle trucks, forty to each. We spent a day and night crammed in them. There was no kind of toilet. We were let out occasionally to take a few steps as exercise. But we were still given no food. Sometimes, when the train stopped, a few German civilians would walk along the trucks and the men tried bartering with them. I thought myself lucky. I was able to offer my leather jacket, a good warm one. In exchange I got a tiny hunk of stale black bread. I preferred to be cold but alive. I would be even colder if I died of starvation.

It seemed almost unbelievable when we arrived at a place called Giessen and met some other prisoners of war. They gave us some white English bread. They had been captured some time ago and were lucky enough to have received parcels from England. But I was soon moved on again to another prisoner of war camp at Kassel. I was now about one hundred and fifty miles inside the German border, to the north of Frankfurt, in the Hessen Region, famous for being the part of

Germany where the Brothers Grimm, Jacob and Wilhelm, collected their fairy tales.

The camp at Kassel was huge. It held soldiers of all nationalities, English, Italian, French. As soon as we arrived we had to report to a small reception centre and an English prisoner of war working there whispered to me, "They'll bloody well kill you, here."

And they very nearly did.

During the whole of the six weeks I was there, the only food I had to eat was one small slice of black bread, doled out each morning, although I always had plenty of water to drink. The bread was brought to the camp each day by train. Like every other inmate, I was intent on being a member of the squad that unloaded it. The individual loaves were passed along the line of men, from hand to hand. Like the others, I tried to do this as slowly as possible. Hanging on to each loaf as long as I dared, so my fingers nails would have time to dig out a tiny morsel of bread from the bottom.

I remember two remarkable things happened while I was at the camp. The most remarkable one for me, personally, being I had a shower. I remember it was Easter Monday. At the time I could not have named the last day I even rinsed my hands and face properly. We new arrivals were lined up, marched outside the camp and taken in groups of twenty into a big hut. I was told to strip and put my clothes on a big metal ring, which was taken away.

I had to line up in a queue and wait. Then one of the two Russian prisoners of war shaved off every hair on my body. He started with my head. Pressing the razor at the back of my neck and going up and over the top of it in one smooth stroke. Only when he reached my forehead did he lift the razor away from my skull. He repeated the action until I was totally bald. By the time he had finished I had not got a single hair left anywhere on my body. I was told to rub blue ointment everywhere the hair had been. After that, we all stood under the shower together, tall, short, thin, broad. The water was hot, but we lacked soap, so I had to rub the dirt off with my hands. After a final dousing with cold water at the end, we all ran pretty smartly up and down the room to try to stop ourselves shivering. Fortunately, my clothes had been baked to fumigate them and I found they were still lovely and warm when I got dressed. I remember how heavily it snowed as we were marched back to the camp.

The second remarkable thing that happened was Field Marshal von Hindenburg, one of Germany's top Generals, visited the camp. We had no idea he was coming. Just before he arrived, we were told to come out of our huts and line up on parade. Then the Field Marshal, done up in his German army dress uniform, a gleaming pointed helmet on his head, all his medals on display on his chest, proceeded to inspect us. Escorting him was a high ranking British officer.

Our lines were divided into sections with an English officer in charge of each. Just before the Field Marshal inspected a section, the English officer in charge would order the men to stand to attention. It was a mark of respect for a high-ranking fellow soldier, even if he were fighting on the other side. When my section, in turn, was asked to stand to attention, everyone did so except one Canadian soldier standing near me. When Field Marshal von Hindenburg, reached the Canadian, the English officer again ordered the soldier to stand to attention. But he still refused, saying defiantly, "He's not my Governor, so I'm not standing to attention".

You could not hear anyone even breath after he said that. But the German Field Marshal simply put out his hand, patted him on the shoulder and said quietly to him in English, "Well done, well done".

One Monday morning I was ordered to report to the guardroom. I joined two other prisoners of war already waiting there. I never knew why the three of us were picked out from the others. An armed guard took us, by train, to Kirchhain, about fifteen miles from Kassel. A short stout man met us at the railway station there. I gathered he was a Dr Kleam. His English was not very good, so when he spoke to the three of us, I did not realise at first what he wanted. Finally, he used his hands to show us and then I understood. He was asking if any of us could milk a cow. I nodded and he indicated he would have me. It seemed he had been given first choice. The three of us then left Dr Kleam and, still accompanied by our German guard, got on another train. This took us to a small village not far from Kirchhain, called Amoneburg.

Amoneburg, I discovered, was an old village full of timbered houses. Built on high ground, it had wonderful views over the surrounding countryside, laid out with a network of small fields. The village was not big enough to have its own proper railway station. The train simply halted for a few minutes and the four of us jumped off. Our guard marched the three of us down a hill and when we reached the mill at the bottom, he handed one of my mates over to the miller. He was to work for him. Then the guard, my one remaining mate and myself marched back up the hill. I noticed the trees lining the road were filled with apple blossom, a delightful sight. It reminded me of home.

A German soldier, gathering walnut tree leaves, waved to us and called out something. But I did not understand a word he said. I spoke no German then. Our guard took the two of us to a building that, if I had been in England, I would have said looked like the village hall. But, whatever it might have been in peacetime, this was wartime. Now, surrounded by a tall barbed wire fence, it was serving as a miniature prisoner of war camp. It housed allied soldiers from several countries. I cheered up a little when some of the French gave us a few small pieces of bread and corned beef from their Red Cross parcels.

After finishing our meal, the other English soldier and myself were taken to a farm and the guard handed the other prisoner of war over to the farmer. Then the guard walked me into the centre of the village and we went into a baker's shop. The woman behind the counter, wearing a long white apron, looked about forty to forty-five and was a bit on the plump side. She spoke a little English and I gathered she was Frau Kleam, wife of the man I had met at the railway station in Kirchhain. I never saw her husband, Dr Kleam again.

Perhaps he was sent away somewhere to do work connected with the war.

The guard handed Frau Kleam a set of documents and she beckoned me through to a room at the back of the shop. Having asked if I were hungry, to which I replied yes, she cut a thick crust from a loaf of black bread. Then she cut two further thick slices. She gave me the two pieces of bread, put a big bowl of jam on the table, and indicated I should sit in one of the chairs beside it and help myself. Then Frau Kleam went back into the shop to sign the papers confirming I had been handed safely over to her.

In the few minutes Frau Kleam was out of the room, I ate both the slices of bread and the crust. When she returned she did not say a word. She simply handed me the loaf and the knife for me to help myself to more. But two thick slices and the crust were enough, for the moment, even for me. Several times, Frau Kleam tried to persuade me to move to a more comfortable chair. But she failed. I felt so uneasy. I could not relax. I could hardly believe I was here, with a German woman, in a German house, in a German village. Somehow, it did not feel right for me to be sitting back in a comfortable German armchair. Not when our two countries were fighting each other.

Frau Kleam kept telling me, "Varter come soon. Varter come soon."

Her father, Herr Joseph Weitzel (he looked at least seventy), did arrive a short time later. He asked me several questions, in German. But as I knew nothing of the language, I did not understand him. Later, I realised he was asking me if I were strong. And could I really milk a cow. As he illustrated this last remark with a movement of his hands, like Dr Kleam. I was able to nod yes. Herr Weitzel took me to a shed, a sort of barn really, at the back of the baker's shop and handed me a bucket. It was only a small shed. Three cows were in one corner and it was a really tight squeeze for me to get in between them to milk them. But it did not take long. To my surprise, I only got what I judged to be just over two pints of milk from the three of them. I was to find out the reason for their low yield later.

I took the milk into the house and Frau Kleam indicated I should wash my hands and come and sit down at the dining table. On the highly polished top, minus a cloth, was a big dish of boiled potatoes and another of sour milk. Laid out nearby were three plates, three spoons and three forks. I had no idea what I should do with my two implements, but Frau Kleam showed me the correct procedure. You held your spoon in your left hand and your fork in your right. You speared a piece of potato with your fork, scooped up a portion of sour milk in your spoon, dunked the piece of potato in the sour milk in your spoon and ate it. I had never had sour milk before and did not think much of it, when I tasted it. Herr Weitzel seemed very surprised I did not like it very much. But since any sort of food was welcome, I ate it. I must confess, I felt even more uneasy and uncomfortable now. Somehow, I felt it was even more wrong for me to be sitting there, eating a meal with two Germans, when our two countries were at war.

After our meal, Herr Weitzel said something that sounded like "barracks". A moment or two later his young grandson arrived. I learned later he was ten years old and lived elsewhere in the village. Apparently, he would escort me back to the "barracks", the building with the barbed wire fence. I was to work at the bakers during the day and sleep in the "barracks" at night. Herr Weitzel's grandson would show me the way back to the "barracks" tonight only because I did not know the way. The young boy took his job very seriously. He marched solemnly along beside me, his wooden toy rifle propped firmly on his shoulder.

When I got back, I discovered the other two men who had come to Amoneburg with me, had not been so lucky. They had not been given a lot of food. Unfortunately, I had eaten a bit too much. And for me, it was the wrong kind of food. I had no bed and a Frenchman offered to share his with me. But not long into the night, I began to feel the effects of the sour milk on my stomach. I was in agony. A big barrel in the corner of our room acted as a latrine. It was quite a job to hitch yourself up and balance on the top. But I was up and down on it frequently during the night. The Frenchman was none too pleased.

CHAPTER
SIXTEEN

Next morning, I made my own way to the baker's shop. I arrived at the back door at seven o'clock and Herr Weitzel gave me some coffee before I milked the cows. Then he took me across to a big heap of wood lying on the opposite side of the road. I had to split the three-foot long pieces, using a wedge and wooden mallet. The wood was needed to feed the fire that heated the oven in the baker's shop.

The wood was lying just outside a small guesthouse. I had not been working long before I spotted a young girl, about seventeen, peeping out at me from behind the guesthouse door. She was a good-looking girl, slim with blue eyes and lovely long blonde hair tied in two plaits. I thought she must be secretly laughing at me, a foreign prisoner of war, having to do whatever work he was given. Feeling embarrassed and humiliated, I started muttering to myself. But in a little while she moved outside, stood beside me and said, "Good morning" in English. I lifted my cap, given to me by Herr Weitzel, and responded politely with the same phrase, but added "Miss" on the end. Almost in a whisper, she asked me how I was faring for food. She spoke quite reasonable English. I told her I was doing all right but my two friends were not doing so well. She offered to hide a loaf of bread in the shed at the back of the guesthouse that evening. Almost all the houses appeared to have some sort of shed or barn at the back with animals in them. The girl said her name was Gretchen and that in English it meant Margaret. But her father appeared and beckoned her to go indoors and that put an end to our conversation.

I split wood all morning until Herr Weitzel, who had spent the time baking bread, called me in for a midday meal of coffee, bread, jam and cake. Afterwards, he told me to get out the wagon. I was very surprised. I had not seen any horses about. But we went round the back to his shed and I got the wagon out. Then Herr Weitzel led out one of the cows. He talked to her all the time, in German of course, and she was most obedient, moving quietly along beside him. Herr Weitzel indicated I should bring out the next one. So I went into the shed. The only thing I could think of to say to her was, "Gee up". But the cow remained exactly where she was. Obviously, she did not understand English. In fact, she refused to move a step until Herr Weitzel came and spoke to her in German. Then she slowly strolled out. I hooked the two cows to the shafts of the wagon and Herr Weitzel produced two headpieces and fitted them over their horns. These were to help control and direct them. But I found out later that, most times, the cows reacted better to verbal instruction, provided these were in German, of course.

Herr Weitzel seated himself at the front of the wagon and I walked behind. The wagon moved slowly away along the street, its wheels pitching jerkily over the uneven cobblestones that lined it. We started to go down the hill and the weight of the wagon pressing forward became almost too much for the cows to hold. Turning, Herr Weitzel pointed to a lever at the back, waving his hand to show I should move it. This must be the brake I thought. I slammed the lever over hard and the wagon stopped dead. "Schweinhund, dumkopf, oxcup," were some of the words Herr Weitzel shrieked at me. Hurriedly, I pushed the lever back to its original position and we started off again. But soon Herr Weitzel waved his hand at me a second time. I slammed the lever over. The wagon stopped dead. Herr Weitzel shrieked at me. The same thing happened again. And again. And again. Each time Herr Weitzel shrieked the same words at me. He kept yelling instructions at me louder and louder. But, all of them being in German, I did not understand anything he said. Eventually, I realised the trick was to judge exactly how far the lever needed to be moved over. I had to apply just sufficient pressure on the brake to stop the wagon going forward faster than the cows could manage. Too much pressure and it stopped moving altogether.

Eventually, when the wagon arrived at Herr Weitzel's two acres of land at the bottom of the hill, he showed me a set of harrows, iron frames with large teeth. These break up the ground when the harrows are pulled along. I had to load the harrows onto the wagon. Then we went on to a further two acres he owned, about a quarter of a mile away.

There, I unloaded the wagon and Herr Weitzel indicated he wanted me to release the cows from it and hook them up to the harrows. I was amazed. Chemin and Bless ploughing. I knew the cows' names by now. One was brown, the other a creamy white. I discovered that between them, the two did most of the farm work. Herr Weitzel spoke quietly to the cows. In German. And they began to pull the harrows up and down the field. He walked at the front leading them. I walked along beside him. Then he stopped and indicated I should lead them. But the cows refused to take one single step with me. He had to speak to them in German again, before they would move on. So, nervously, I set off with the two cows on my own, minus Herr Weitzel. But, halfway down the field Chemin and Bless seemed to sense I was by myself with them because they bolted, lured away from their ploughing by a patch of long inviting grass at the far side of the field. Herr Weitzel rushed over and gave them both such a hiding. He used a big long stick with a nail hammered through the end. They were a bit more obedient after that. When I finished ploughing, I hitched the cows to the wagon and we went back to the bakery. Again I was given a pail and told to milk the three of them. This time I was not surprised when I did not get very much. The cows were not kept simply for their milk as dairy cattle were in England. They were working animals. After that I had what turned out to be, more often than not, my usual evening meal, sour cream and potatoes. Like England, food was now very scarce in Germany.

I left the bakery at about eight o'clock to go back to the barracks and found Margaret outside. I always preferred to call her by her English name. She called me Johann. She told me she wanted to improve her English. I told her I wanted to learn German. We stood and talked for a little while. Afterwards I checked the shed at the back of her home. The loaf she had promised me was there. I walked back to the camp with it hidden under my jacket and shared it with my two friends. They said they had not done very well for food again.

From then on, I had a regular work routine. I milked the cows and worked in the fields by myself, once I had learned how to handle Chemin and Bless. Sometimes, if Herr Weitzel felt so inclined, I kneaded the dark brown dough he baked every day, pushing and pulling it about for around half an hour.

Margaret waited for me every evening outside the bakery and continued to leave a loaf for me in the shed. Then I used to meet her again later. The French and the Italians had different guards. We three English prisoners were treated more leniently by ours. They allowed us to go out at night to stroll round the village. We made sure we kept them sweet. We passed them regular handouts from our Red Cross parcels. A tin of soup was an especially pleasing present. But most of the things in my parcels, particularly the chocolate, went to Margaret. We were beginning to get very attached to each other. She gave me another cap and an old overcoat. But about two months later, Margaret's father, Herr Ludwig von Creipe, stopped me in the street and told me never to go near the shed at the back of his house again. Obviously he was not keen on his daughter associating with an enemy soldier.

But Herr von Creipe also had a two-acre field. His field was right next to Herr Weitzel's. And, just as in England, there were no young men available to work the land. That was why I had been allocated to Herr Weitzel. Maybe anyone connected with producing food got prisoner of war labour. I had cut down Herr Weitzel's hay crop with a scythe and was ready to turn it, when Herr von Creipe offered a suggestion. If I helped Margaret turn his hay, she would help me turn Herr Weitzel's. Apparently, he did not mind us being together if we were working. But he still objected to there being any social contact between us.

So the two of us began turning the hay together. One of the days we were working it was very hot. Margaret had brought coffee and cake with her. We finished turning the hay and sat down on the grass and had the coffee and cake. Then, Margaret said she was going for a swim in the stream running by the end of the field. She asked if I were coming in the water as well. I said no, because I had not got a swimming costume. She answered in German that it did not matter. She undressed and dived into the water. I stayed where I was. I did not want to get into trouble. I was a foreign soldier. An enemy soldier. I thought of the two "squaddies" the German soldiers had shot. They had done nothing to deserve it. If I did something to deserve it, I would certainly get shot. But, eventually, I did go in the water with her. Next day, Herr von Creipe took me aside and spoke to me. He emphasised he did not want me associating socially with Margaret again. He still did not mind if it involved work, but we were never ever to socialise as friends. All we could do, from then on, was wave to each other across the street and secretly write letters. A young fourteen-year old lad she knew acted as delivery boy. He used to leave mine in the shed at the back of her home.

At the end of July it was harvest time. I had to gather in all the rye, essential for making the black bread. I walked along cutting it down with a big scythe. An old German woman followed behind me. She carried a sickle in her right hand and with this she collected up the rye and pushed it into a bundle. Her left arm supported the bundle until it was big enough to lay aside. Then I came along and tied up all the bundles.

Next, the rye had to be thrashed. We did this in the barn. We put a couple of bundles on the floor on a sheet and the three of us, a German man, Margaret and myself, thrashed them with thrails. These were long wooden sticks with leather bound round the beating end. As it was work, Margaret's father approved of us being together. He did not have much choice really because there was no other man to do it.

I had to hold my thrail with both hands, lift it high above my head and bring it down hard on the rye. Then I had to swing it up above my head again, immediately. The idea was to work to a steady rhythm, up, down, up, down, up, down. But the up and down movement of my thrail had to fit in with the up and down movements made by the other two. The ends of our three thrails had to hit the rye one after the other. So each of us had to bring our thrails down in the same order every time, otherwise we would just keep crashing them together. It took me a long time to get the right rhythm and keep to it. At first, I kept swinging my thrail up too high so the end dipped down behind me and I hit myself on the back of the head. But, at last, with Herr Weitzel standing beside me, patiently counting ein, zwei, drei, ein, zwei, drei, ein, zwei, drei, over and over again, I finally succeeded.

After we had finished thrashing a batch of rye, we removed all the straw. Then the three of us knelt down beside the grain we had extracted and started to blow on it. We blew and blew and blew, trying to disperse as much of the lighter chaff, the husk, as we could. Afterwards we shovelled the grain into sacks. We carried on like this until all the bundles of rye had been thrashed. The next time I thrashed grain I did it alone and in secret. Because it was corn and Herr Weitzel did not want the German authorities to know about it. You were supposed to give them most of the grain you grew. You were only allowed to keep a tiny percentage back for yourself. So the corn had to be smuggled up to the shed behind the shop after dark. This time I used an old machine to do the thrashing. I had to pour plenty of water into it, pile a big heap of wood in the special place for a fire, then keep fanning away at this with a piece of paper to make sure it caught alight. After that I had to sit down and wait quite a time for the steam to get up. The hardest work I ever did in my life, I did after I had thrashed that corn. I had to haul the heavy sacks of grain up to Herr Weitzel's loft to hide them away there safely. Both Herr Weitzel and Frau Kleam were too old to help me. I was the only one who could do it.

As well as hiding corn away, Herr Weitzel had another secret. He kept a pig. It was hidden away at the back of the shed. The Germans were especially short of meat. So all animals belonging to private citizens were supposed to be handed over to the authorities when they were ready for slaughter. They kept most of the meat and only gave just a tiny portion back to the owner. One day, Herr Weitzel whispered a question to me. Would I help him kill his pig? Naturally, I said yes.

That evening, we waited until it was dark. Then we tied a piece of string to one of the pig's back legs and quickly herded it along the street to the elderly butcher's shop, two doors away. The butcher was waiting. He was holding an axe in one hand and a long sharp knife in the other. Giving the knife to me, he lifted the axe and whacked it down hard on the pig's head. Down the pig went. My job was immediately to dig the knife into the place the butcher indicated on its body. As it happened, the pig had been standing over a drain. As soon as Herr Weitzel saw the pig's blood was beginning to run down the drain, he rushed for a bowl, so he could collect it in that instead. He even tried to scoop up with his fingers, the small amount already congealing, on the floor.

We quickly strung up the dead pig by its two back legs, hiding it away in the back of the shop, where no-one would find it. If anyone discovered we had killed it, the butcher and Herr Weitzel faced a heavy fine. The next night, I went back to the butcher's shop and helped him cut up the pig. Not a sliver from it was wasted. I put the eyes, ears, insides and tail through a sausage machine. The intestines acted as sausage skins. The liver was made into liver pâté. I think most of the meat must have been hoarded away somewhere, because I only ever saw one joint afterwards.

When autumn arrived and all the harvest had been gathered in, it was usual for the ploughing to begin again. I had an exciting, if painful, experience one day when I was doing this. The plough was taken down to the fields on a sort of two-wheeled trolley. Chemin and Bless pulled it along. The two cows were also to pull the plough. I had hitched them up and was ploughing away, when I went over a wasps' nest. Did the wasps pour out! They attacked Chemin and Bless and the pair of them went berserk. The cows bolted. Somehow, they managed to swing the plough against a nearby apple tree and the jolt disconnected the chains binding them to it. Away they careered. Heading for home. A short while later, an anxious Herr Weitzel brought them back, worried as to why they were running free. I had been stung all over my head and was in such agony, I could hardly speak to him.

That was not the only little accident I had. One day I cut my finger while I was working in the fields. It became infected and very painful. So Herr Weitzel took me to the doctor. He lanced it, bandaged it up and suggested I should rest my hand for a day or so. It meant I could do very little work. I could not hang around the baker's shop all day, so I used to go and lie down on the straw in the shed. The shed contained the family's only toilet, a big box with a hole in the top. One afternoon I was lying in the straw and must have nodded off, because when I opened my eyes, Frau Kleam was sitting on it. At that moment, although I tried not to, I coughed. She told me, in German, she did not know I was there. She did not seem at all put out. I answered in the same language, saying it did not matter.

All the animal and human solid waste was shovelled into a big heap, at the side of the shed. It stayed there until it could be loaded on a wagon and taken down to the fields to be spread on them. It was a cheap and effective fertilizer. Everyone did the same. No one seemed to mind having piles of the stuff so close to the houses. The urine drained into a big tank and was also used as a form of manure on the fields.

CHAPTER
SEVENTEEN

Eventually, rumours about the war began to filter round the "barracks". The fighting was supposed to be almost over, but our Red Cross parcels were still arriving and one day we were told a few were waiting for us at Kassel. For some reason, they could not be moved on from there to Amoneburg. Someone would have to go and get them. One of the French prisoners of war, an officer, I think, because he was very smartly dressed, had been given the task of organising their collection. To my surprise, he chose me to go with him. He spoke good English.

Kassel was only about half an hour away by train. But the French officer said we could not possibly go there, collect the parcels and get back in one day. He insisted the two of us must spend the night at a guesthouse in the town. We were clean and free from lice. But we might not be either of those if we had to sleep at the big prisoner of war camp in the town, the same camp where I had spent my first six weeks of captivity, had a shower and seen Field Marshal von Hindenburg. Even if the arrangement were agreed, I wondered how we were going to manage. I had no money. I had nothing to show who I was if challenged.

But the Frenchman told me not to worry. We would both be in our prisoner of war uniform. Perhaps he had quietly been given money and some official papers authorising us to move about in the area.

We got to Kassel, found a room in a guesthouse and had tea sent up. It consisted of bread with some sort of fat spread, jam, coffee and cake. Afterwards we took a stroll round the town. Noticing a cinema, the Frenchman suggested we should go inside and see a film. Again I told him I had no money and, again, he said I was not to worry. Of course, we saw a German film. When it ended we heard a loud burst of music and recognised the tune being played as the German National Anthem. Everyone around us immediately jumped up and stood to attention. Automatically, without thinking, I tried to do exactly what they had done. But the Frenchman immediately jerked me back into my seat. The German audience did not seem to mind the two of us remaining seated.

Our bedroom at the guesthouse had quite comfortable single beds, but we had to sleep between thick paper sheets. The slightest movement and they crackled and crackled. The noise went on all night. When we got back to Amoneburg with the parcels, I found the rumours that the war had ended had been confirmed. A notice was pinned up in the camp stating all prisoners of war would be repatriated as soon as possible. Meanwhile, no prisoner was to be insulted or injured in any way. From then on, we all had our personal freedom during the day. But I decided to carry on working at the baker's shop, as there was little else for me to do to occupy my time. Then I heard more good news. An armistice was about to be signed.

A few days later, I left Amoneburg early one morning to take a wagon-load of corn to the miller's at Kirchhain, about one and a half miles away. I was passing the railway station there when a train happened to draw in. Dozens of German soldiers poured out of it into the street. Spotting me in my prisoner of war uniform, they immediately surrounded my wagon and made Chemin and Bless lie down. The two cows were usually very obedient, provided the instructions they were given were in German. At the same time, all the German soldiers kept shouting, "Englander, Englander" at the top of their voices. I was terrified. Had I survived being wounded, had I lived through, possibly, one of the heaviest bombardments of the war, endured a gas attack, not to mention being captured and having to work as a prisoner of war, only to die just as hostilities were formally ending. Then I realised the soldiers were shouting something else. They were pointing to a café just along the street and were telling me to, "Komm" and, "Drinken". It seemed they were as delighted as I was the war was over. When I had not returned to Amoneburg by midday, Herr Weitzel came looking for me. He saw the cows still patiently lying down in the street and heard the hullabaloo coming from the café. He came inside and told me it was time I hurried back. But the German soldiers just laughed and quickly hustled him out. The only thing he could do was to take Chemin and Bless home himself.

About a week later, without any warning, I was told I was being moved back to the big camp at Kassel the next day. It was the first step in my repatriation home. I told Herr Weitzel straight away. I was still banned from going anywhere near Margaret, but Herr Weitzel said she could come over to the baker's shop that evening to say goodbye to me. He went over to the guesthouse to tell her that himself.

Margaret came to the shop that evening. After she left, Herr Weitzel asked me if I would be coming back to marry her. I did not reply. But I had given her the address of Mushroom Hall. Next morning I marched with the other former prisoners of war to Kirchhain, where I caught a train to Kassel. Margaret had promised she would watch her Johann leave Amoneburg. But she did not. Perhaps her father would not let her.

I joined hundreds of other Allied soldiers crammed into the camp at Kassel, all of us eager for news of the next stage of our repatriation. But the days passed and no further information reached us. The longer we continued to be confined there, the more impatient and restless we became. Meanwhile we could see our German guards were becoming more and more agitated and more and more nervous about what might happen if the news we were so avidly expecting was delayed much longer. One afternoon, a large group of us massed in front of the main gate. To be fair, the German officer on duty may have thought we were about to attempt to break out through it. Certainly, from the speedy manner in which he acted, he seemed to be very alert, as though he were anticipating there might be some sort of trouble. And was ready for it. Almost at once, he ordered the guard in the surveillance tower to open fire. Maybe the officer giving the order only intended the guard to shoot over our heads. However, the fact was he fired his machine gun straight into the centre of the group. Several of our boys died right away. Many others were injured. His action enraged every single one of us. But, for some reason, the Australian soldiers felt especially affronted. They, in particular, were adamant they would exact revenge.

That same evening, when it was dark, a large group of us got together and clustered round the base of the surveillance tower. An English cigarette was the bait. We got cigarettes in our Red Cross parcels. No German could resist one. We lit a few and silently started puff, puff, puffing the smoke upwards. Someone quietly called up to the guard asking if "Jerry" wanted a cigarette. We heard the word "Ja" called softly in reply. Cautiously, the guard began to creep down. He looked round carefully, checking to see no German officer was anywhere near. There were none. We had checked carefully, too. A cigarette was held up and offered. The guard's hand reached down for it. Then the Australians hit him on the head with something. His helmet fell off and rolled towards me. I picked it up. At last, I had my souvenir. The helmet had quite a large dent in it. Whatever implement the Australians had used, it must have been very hard. The soldier who first hit him, and the others who kept on hitting the German guard, were powerful fellows. Eventually, the cover of a sewerage drain was hurriedly prised open and the Australians threw the guard, conscious, unconscious or dead, down it. I never heard another word mentioned about him.

Two days later, I marched with other fellow soldiers to Kassel railway station and boarded a train for Holland. I spent my first night there in some sort of large hall. I only had straw to lie on, but I cannot explain the elation I felt as I realised I had finally left Germany. Despite Margaret, for me the country meant heavy bombardments, a gas attack, seeing fellow soldiers shot, prisoner of war camps. The next morning the Dutch gave me fresh homemade bread and coffee. It tasted delicious after our diet of black bread in the camp. I was examined by a doctor at a reception centre and given another English army uniform. It was not a very good fit, but it was in far better condition than the tatty worn out garments I was wearing.

The next day we marched to the docks where we boarded a boat for England. Once we sailed, most of us were seasick. Halfway across the North Sea, the boat got stuck on a sandbank. Looking out over the side, I could see mines floating in the water all around us. The crew were firing at them with rifles to make them explode. I was offered a gun to try my luck, but could not hit one.

Eventually, the tide floated the ship off the sandbank and it sailed on and docked at Hull. I spent two nights in the barracks there, before going on to Bury to be "demobbed". Officially, I was still a member of the Lancashire Fusiliers. After that, I was free to make my way to Essex. I had sent a telegram to my parents, so Mr Pinnock was waiting for me at Brentwood station, with his pony and trap. The same Mr Pinnock, who had given me a lift home, when I was on "agricultural" leave. He gave me news of my father. Sadly, his health had deteriorated further. Despite this, what a reunion I had with my parents, especially my mother. Only now did I realise what an anxious and traumatic time they had experienced. First, an official telegram had arrived saying I was listed as missing believed killed. Then they received the green envelope containing all my private papers. The two of them believed I was dead. It was several months before Edie Curtis, our local post woman, hammered on their bedroom window early one morning and they heard her shouting the news I was alive. She was holding a postcard I had sent from Germany, saying I was a prisoner of war.

I slept extra well that night, knowing I was home. Next morning, someone tapped hard on my bedroom window. I was still fast asleep, but I woke up and opened it. A dear old lady called Mrs Saddler, a neighbour, passed a pot of tea and several slices of hot toast through to me. It really was nice to be back.

CHAPTER
EIGHTEEN

It was, indeed, lovely to be home again. To be back in my own country. But, I discovered, it was not quite the same country I had left behind when I set off to go to war. I believed then that, on my return, I would simply carry on with my life, live exactly the same sort of life I had lived before I went away. My family's circumstances might have changed. I was now living in a different county. But I was still the same person. A little older, but still young. I was healthy. I had served a three-year gardening apprenticeship, so was fully trained. I had gained experience by working as a journeyman. Successfully taken one step up the private country estate employment ladder and become a foreman. I had not foreseen the possibility of there being anything to prevent it.

But I quickly discovered that the real life fact was that nobody seemed to want to employ gardeners now. Not anywhere. Especially locally. Because my father was so ill, I did not want to work very far way. I kept looking in *The Gardeners' Chronicle* but there were almost no jobs available anywhere. As week after week passed, I decided it might be wise to forget my ambitions for a time. Instead of looking forward to the day when I was a Bailiff or Head Gardener on a big estate, it might be better if, temporarily, I took a step back down the promotion ladder. But even though I was willing to work as just an ordinary journeyman, not even details of those jobs were being printed. Private country estates did not seem to want to employ any sort of outdoor staff any more. There were even times when I wondered whether I would ever get another job again.

The only money I had was a small gratuity, given to me when I left the army. It was running out fast and my family and I could not live on the small amount of money we obtained from the animals on the farm. I knew there was only one thing I could do. I hated the idea. I had always believed unemployment happened to other people. That it would never happen to a skilled man like me. But finally, I had to do it. I pedalled into Ongar, a small town about three miles away to "sign on", and I added my signature to the unemployment register. This meant I was entitled to receive "dole" money of ten shillings a week as an unemployment allowance. They made sure I was genuinely unemployed and not earning money doing little jobs on the side by making me cycle into Ongar three times each week to "sign on". Everyone who was unemployed had to present themselves in the same way. No signature on just one of those days meant no "dole" money on the Friday.

I had plenty of time to build a small pond on the farm for the ducks. They had joined the cows, pigs and hens already at Mushroom Hall. I took over responsibility for all the animals and did all the general maintenance work. There was still no one else to do it. Stanley continued to serve abroad with the Hertfordshire Yeomanry. He was not "demobbed" until much later. Alice was living in St Albans with her husband. And William attended the village school. He was still far too young to do anything but the lightest jobs.

Food was still scarce and basic ones such as margarine and sugar were still rationed. You only got a very small amount of these and hardly any meat. Most people supplemented this by keeping tame rabbits to eat. I used to take a gun into the woods and shoot a few wild ones. I came back with the odd pheasant too, although it was illegal to shoot them without a licence. But I was not the only one doing it.

To help pass the time, I went to lectures in the local village hall, given by a Mr Hammett. He told us about the new farm tractors just being introduced into the countryside. He got me on a little training course in Berkshire, a government supported scheme, but it only lasted two weeks. Several letters came from Margaret in Germany. But I did not reply to them. I was too concerned about my father to spend time writing to her. He was gradually getting weaker and beginning to spend more and more time in bed. Finally, our local doctor, Dr Hackney, said my father needed an operation. It had to be done quickly, but hospitals were for those with money, so how was it to be arranged? He contacted a surgeon, Dr Boyce Barrow, living at Writtle, a village six miles away, and he agreed to come to Mushroom Hall and operate. Dr Hackney would be there to assist and a Dr Gough from Brentwood would give the anaesthetic. My father agreed to have it only so long as I stayed with him.

The operation was done in my bedroom. I held my father's hand while the anaesthetic was given to him, and waited until he was asleep. Then Dr Hackney whispered it was time for me to go. He did not have to tell me twice. Two weeks later, my father had a second operation and a cancerous tumour was removed from his stomach. Dr Hackney put it in a jar of preserving spirit. He kept it on the windowsill in his surgery for years. Every time I went to consult him he used to point to it and tell me there was a bit of my poor old Dad.

My father died on a Good Friday. He was only fifty-nine. A local undertaker made the coffin and organised the funeral service at St Nicholas Church in Kelvedon Hatch. Afterwards, his body was taken to St Albans to be buried. On the way there, the hearse broke down and we had to get another one. Sister Etheldreda, Sister Clare and one or two other nuns from the Convent came to his interment. The priest from there also came and sprinkled holy water on his coffin just before it was lowered into the grave.

There was another reason, apart from my father's illness, why I was not replying to Margaret's letters. Soon after I arrived home, while I was still settling in at Mushroom Hall, a young girl from the local village caught my eye. She lived nearby with her aunt at Hatch Farm, a lovely big old house in the centre of the village. I had first seen her playing the organ in the parish church, when I was home on "agricultural" leave. When I returned after the war, I saw her again coming along the lane one afternoon, wearing a very smart red dress. At the time I was already dallying with one or two others, but I asked her to go for a walk with me that evening and she agreed. I had not expected her to say yes. I had to rush away and cancel an existing arrangement for me to go walking with another local girl called Madge McMain.

I started going out regularly with the girl in the red dress. I had very little money. Neither did a lot of other people. But we went to whist drives and dances held in the local village hall and other village halls close by. And to dances in Brentwood. It did not cost much to get in. We travelled around in my parents' pony and trap. All the pubs in Brentwood had stables. They were open to anyone prepared to pay a shilling. Water was available but I had to supply my own food for the horse. I used to put him in one of the stables and leave my trap in the yard. I collected him and the trap after the dance ended at twelve o'clock. I remember on one occasion that for some reason I borrowed a friend's horse. He was a "high stepper" and, once he set off, was reluctant to stop. Then it started to rain. He did not like that at all. He bolted and we shot round several corners on two wheels before, eventually, he quietened down. As well as going to dances, I was playing cricket again. As captain of the Kelvedon Hatch village team, I played against those from all the surrounding villages, Blackmore, Doddinghurst, Navestock.

150

Two years passed since I had left the army and I was still without a job. Then I spotted an advertisement in the local newspaper. A position was offered on a small private country estate, about three quarters of a mile away, on the outskirts of the next village, Stondon Massey. It was only a very small estate. But a job was a job. And the vacancy advertised was for a Head Gardener.

Hoping to prove I was the right man for the job, I carefully folded my references from Porters Park and Warren House, slipped them in my pocket and walked down the lanes to Chivers, the "big house" mentioned in the advertisement. It did not seem to be all that big but naturally I went round and knocked on the back door. The parlour maid came to the door and I explained I had come about the job and showed her my references. She said she thought the position had already been filled, but offered to take them to the owner, a Mrs Cavalier-Smith. The owner herself then came to the back door and told me the post was no longer available. They were the words I was expecting to hear. There were plenty of unemployed men in the area. Some of them must be equally or even more experienced gardeners than me. Very disappointed, I turned to leave saying, in that case, there was no point in me wasting any more of her time or my own. To my surprise she suddenly said I could have the job, after all. I was overjoyed.

Mrs Cavalier-Smith never told me why she suddenly changed her mind. I was asked how much money I expected to be paid. I knew an ordinary farm worker was earning one pound seven shillings and sixpence each week. Very daringly, I asked for two pounds. I tried to make sure I got it by saying I could not possibly consider anything less, a considerable bluff on my part. But my father had been dead for some time now and I had to help support my mother. Also, I was getting married in a fortnight. My romance with the girl in the red dress had been developing and she was my bride-to-be. I had no job and no prospects of one when we arranged our wedding date. Our only other option was to wait until I had one. But we decided we might go on waiting forever for one to turn up. To my delight, Mrs Cavalier-Smith told me to start work the following Monday. Her present Head Gardener was old and wanted to retire. I could hardly believe it. I had not only got a job. I had got a top one. Only on a very small estate, true, but I had achieved my ambition. I was now a Head Gardener. At the end of my first week, Mrs Cavalier-Smith gave me ten shillings as a wedding present. The second week, I spent a few days away at Southend-on-Sea on my honeymoon. When I got back, she gave me a full week's wages so at the weekend my wife and I popped back there again for another two days,

I still had Margaret's letters. The first thing my wife did after we were married was to tear them up

Mrs Cavalier-Smith, an American lady of Dutch descent, had been born Maria Gibson Smith. She was about fifty-nine years of age when I joined her staff. She had worked with the Red Cross during the war and was well-known and accepted socially. She had no family in England but entertained a great deal. She was always smartly dressed and walked the mile and a half to church every Sunday until she was seventy. Only then did she use the car. I thought Mrs Cavalier-Smith was an attractive, intelligent, energetic woman. A keen horticulturist, she often worked alongside me in the gardens. Eventually she confided that her husband, also an American, had run away with her best friend less than two years before. I don't think she ever really got over it. Apparently, she had deserted her first husband to marry him. I could recall having seen her second husband, once or twice, driving a horse and trap around the lanes, as fast as the devil. He was the first person in the area to have a motorcar, a Mercedes.

Mrs Cavalier-Smith was a wealthy lady. Her property in England consisted of her house, the surrounding thirty acres with one or two cottages plus a farm with a further fifty acres, which was rented out. When compared with other "big houses", Chivers was a comparatively modest home. It had been built only thirty years before on the instructions of a Mrs Baker, to replace an ancient farmhouse she owned on the site. The new house retained the name of the old one it replaced. The word Chivers was said to have come, originally, from an old local family called Chevers, whose name, in turn, was supposed to have been derived from the French word for goat. Mrs Baker, as the then Lord of the Manor, held a ceremonial old style manorial court in her new home, shortly after it was completed.

Chivers had a large morning room on the first floor. It faced west. You got lovely views of the sunset from there. A bathroom and a separate toilet were also on the first floor. Mrs Cavalier-Smith allowed her staff to use the bathroom, but not the toilet. They had to use an outdoor one. A large round stove, fed with anthracite in winter, stood on the landing. Staff used a small back staircase to get to the first floor. Mrs Cavalier-Smith and her visitors went up and down a much grander one at the front. The house had five main bedrooms and two further ones at the back, along a small passage. One of these was the cook's room. The parlour maid, housemaid and kitchen maid shared the other. The four of them made up Mrs Cavalier-Smith's indoor staff. A woman came in to do the washing, such as sheets. Another, named Mrs Mills, looked after Mrs Cavalier-Smith's personal items. She called at the house each week and wheeled them away in a large pram, to be washed at her home.

An anthracite stove stood in the big hall downstairs. The large dining and drawing rooms, both with a pair of big bay windows in each, opened off this. Cupboards lined a smaller hall at the back of the house. A gunroom, fully equipped with several types of sporting guns, lead off this. There was a kitchen, scullery, parlour maid's pantry and stairs to a cellar, where all the drinks were stored. Mrs Cavalier Smith always kept the keys to the cellar herself, but later she entrusted them to me.

Outside, there were a set of horseboxes and a harness room. The garage, big enough for her two cars, had a

154

flat above it. At the time, Mrs Cavalier-Smith owned a Sunbeam and a Mercedes. The carbide acetylene lamps at the front of the Mercedes had to be lit by hand. Her chauffeur, Fred Oxford, lived in Blackmore, a village two miles north of Stondon Massey. When he was on duty, he wore a navy blue uniform with a peaked cap. His double-breasted coat had two rows of very shiny silver buttons. I remember, at the time, the house was lit by gas. We had to put petrol in an engine in the back yard and wind up a set of weights. As the weights went down the machine provided the gas. We used to wind the weights every morning in winter and every second or third day in the summer. A man used to come down from London twice a year to overhaul the machine and check it was in full working order.

Mrs Cavalier-Smith employed three other gardening staff, in addition to myself. Two of them were trained gardeners. One worked in the kitchen garden and orchard. Another looked after the "pleasure gardens". The third was the "odd job" man. He did any extra work required, anywhere at any time. The gardens contained a large ornamental pond, quite a few rockeries, a rose pagoda and lots of rhododendrons. Once a year in the spring, Mrs Cavalier-Smith used to open the grounds of Chivers to the public, in aid of the local community hospital. I had to sit by the gate and take the money, sixpence per family.

My wife and I began married life in two rooms in Mushroom Hall, but my mother wanted to leave the house. She could not bear to go on living there without my father. Stanley was now a hairdresser and working in Ilford, some miles to the west of Brentwood, on the outskirts of London. He had a customer who believed country air might be the cure for his asthma. So an exchange was arranged. My mother and my brothers Stanley and William, who had ambitions to become an electronics engineer, went to live in the man's home in Ilford. The man came to share Mushroom Hall with my wife and myself. But soon she was expecting our first child and the man's constant coughing throughout the night was keeping her awake. Eventually he died of tuberculosis.

I had plenty of cheek in those days, so I told Mrs Cavalier-Smith it was usual for the owners of private country estates to provide their Head Gardener with a home. I said if she could not do so I would have to leave. Again, a bit of bluff on my part. She found us a place, a small wooden bungalow owned by the local vicar. But neither my wife nor myself liked it. It was dilapidated and uncomfortable. So I went back to Mrs Cavalier-Smith. I pointed out to her, again, that it was the tradition on English private country estates for decent houses to be provided for staff. She decided to build a pair of semi-detached cottages on the border of her land, where two lanes met. Although we moved only about half mile, officially, we left the parish of Kelvedon Hatch. Our new home was just inside the boundary of the Stondon Massey parish.

My wife and I called the semi-detached cottage we lived in Chivers Cottage. The chauffeur lived in the other one. My wife and I were very happy there. Later, just before my wife had our third child, Mrs

Cavalier-Smith built a larger detached cottage for me, just a little way along the lane. This one we called Chivers Lodge. Only a short stretch of rhododendron bushes, running parallel with the lane, separated it from Chivers itself. By taking the little path through them, I could walk there in just a few minutes, whenever Mrs Cavalier Smith needed me.

In the same year I was married and got a job, I got together with Dr Hackney, the doctor who had arranged the operation on my father and we decided to form an ex-servicemen's club. November the eleventh, designated as Armistice Day, was approaching. It appeared an ideal time to get people interested in the idea. I went to see Canon Reeve, Rector of Stondon Massey parish church, St. Peter and St. Paul's. He said he would be delighted to hold a special service, but doubted if I would be able to persuade many ex-servicemen to attend. I told the Rector to leave that to me.

On Armistice Day, over a hundred of us ex-servicemen gathered in front of the pub, The Bricklayers Arms, in the centre of Stondon Massey. Then, in formation, we marched the two miles to St. Peter and St. Paul's Church. It was that distance outside the village. I left the other men at the church gate as I had to sing in the choir. After the service, we all marched to Stondon Hall, a lovely big old house and the home of Captain Fane. We had coffee then held a meeting in the ballroom there.

We formally decided to band together with the aim of forming an ex-service men's club. We elected a committee with me as secretary. It met regularly at my home to organise the collection of members' subscriptions and arrange fundraising events. A Grand Christmas Draw brought in eighty pounds. Eventually a Mr Allen, the owner of a small garage at a place called Tipps Cross in Stondon Massey, offered us the use of an adjacent field at a peppercorn rent. We raised two hundred pounds over four years, sufficient to build a small wooden hall with a corrugated iron roof. This became the official home of the Stondon Massey and District Ex-Service men's club.

The club was very successful. It attracted a large membership and regularly held well-attended social events. Then the current chairman, a Mr Lovegrove, owner of a furniture factory, had to leave the district. He bought the land on which the hall stood, for twenty-five pounds and gave it to the club as a parting present. So trustees were appointed to safeguard the hall's future. By this time I was chairman of the organising committee, so I also became Chairman of the Trustees.

CHAPTER
NINETEEN

By the time I had been working for Mrs Cavalier-Smith for six or seven years, I was no longer just her Head Gardener, employed simply to supervise the outdoor staff. I was also doing the duties of a steward and a secretary as well. I kept all the estate accounts in order. I collected the rents from the farm and cottages. I was responsible for paying all the bills, and paying the staff their wages. I checked over all her financial correspondence from America. She had inherited quite a lot of real estate in Philadelphia. I learnt she was getting the equivalent of five hundred pounds a month from this, a considerable sum in those days.

In order to retain her American citizenship Mrs Cavalier-Smith had to make regular visits to the United States. So she went there every year. She used to travel to America during the last week of October, going by sea, usually on the *Aquitania* or the *Mauretania*, her favourite ships. Only myself and the chauffeur, who worked in the garden during the time she was away, were kept on and paid. The rest of the staff were laid off for the three months she was away. I was left in sole charge of her house, Chivers. She used to write me a letter every week.

When Mrs Cavalier-Smith came back from America, she usually went to take the waters at Bath for three or four weeks from about mid-February through to March. She liked to visit the city again later in the year, in August. Each time she went to America or Bath, I had to collect up all her silver cutlery, silver tea service and other small silver items, pack them in a big case, and deposit the case in the Brentwood branch of the National Westminster Bank for safekeeping.

Then Mrs Cavalier-Smith bought the old farmhouse on the opposite side of the lane to Chivers. The owner, a retired grocer, could no longer afford to keep it. He knew Mrs Cavalier-Smith was a wealthy woman and was going to do his best to make sure she bought it. And paid the top price for it, too. So he threatened to use the farm's ten acres of land to store caravans, knowing this would not have pleased her at all. So Mrs Cavalier Smith gave him one thousand pounds for the farm. She also bought other surrounding fields in the area, aware that if she controlled the land she could prevent any unpleasant intrusive use by outsiders. This meant I had even more to do. Now, in addition to the work I was already doing, I had to collect rent from the new tenant of the farmhouse, arrange for any repairs to be done and collect rent for the extra fields, which were let out for grazing.

But during the many years I worked for her, Mrs Cavalier-Smith did show her appreciation for my help in several ways. She was a member of the Zoological Society. As a member, once a year she was invited to pay a visit to London Zoo. She always used to ask my wife and myself to go there with her. The chauffeur drove the three of us up to London. Mrs Cavalier-Smith paid the zoo's entrance fees for me and my wife. Then she gave us a pound each and we were left to wander round the zoo together while she went off to Harrods, her favourite store. She used to buy everything she needed from Harrods, including brandy and whisky and all her groceries. One of their vans delivered goods to Chivers almost every week.

Mrs Cavalier-Smith was also a member of the Royal Horticultural Society. Every month, she and I used to go to their horticultural shows. Sometimes my wife went too. The chauffeur drove us to Brentwood station and we took the train up to London, arriving by taxi at Harrods, just in time for lunch. It was guaranteed to be an excellent one. Then we would do some shopping in the store. Mrs Cavalier-Smith always bought sugared almonds. She loved sugared almonds. She kept giving boxes of them to my wife.

Mrs Cavalier-Smith always received tickets for the first day of the Chelsea flower show. Sometimes she and I went to it together. Sometimes she gave me the tickets so I could go with my wife. Those times she always handed me a five-pound note as well, so we could buy ourselves a good lunch. One such visit I will never forget. I was wandering along admiring the exhibits when I happened to notice a particularly fine specimen in full bloom. I stepped back to get a wider more general view and felt my heel come down hard on the toe of the man, who happened to be standing behind me. Of course I turned round at once and apologised. The man seemed quite unperturbed. In a very deep, but pleasant voice he merely said, "That's all right, old boy."

I suddenly realised the crowd around me had become unusually quiet. So quiet, I could clearly hear the words being whispered from one to the other, "He stood on the Prince of Wales's toe."

I moved myself somewhere else right away.

After I had been working at Chivers for some time and Mrs Cavalier-Smith had gone to Bath as usual, I got a letter from her asking my wife and myself to visit her there, for a week. We would not be staying at the same hotel, but we would be taking our evening meals with her. Naturally, we accepted her invitation. We arranged for the children to stay with relatives and set off in my Morris Eight. The car was a present from Mrs Cavalier-Smith. I already had a small one of my own, but it could only seat two comfortably, although it did have an extra small "dicky" seat at the back. That vehicle had only cost me five pounds. But Mrs Cavalier-Smith liked me to take her out for a drive occasionally, so she had bought me a more comfortable car, the Morris Eight. As she got older she seemed to prefer the informality of a car smaller than the two rather grand ones she owned.

The particular morning my wife and I were heading for Bath it was very foggy. I got to Hendon and found a traffic jam at the lights there. Traffic lights were a real novelty then. A lorry hemmed me in and when, finally, I managed to get past the lights, a policeman stopped me and said I had come through on red. I told him I did not think I had. Later, I received a summons and although Mrs Cavalier-Smith referred the matter to the A.A., I was fined two pounds.

The hotel where Mrs Cavalier-Smith stayed was a really lovely one. It was high up on a hill. For the evening meal I always wore a proper dinner jacket and Mrs Cavalier-Smith checked my bow tie before we went into the dining room. I remember being mystified at first by the waiters' suggestion that we have "sooty" potatoes.

The following year, my wife and myself visited Mrs Cavalier-Smith at Bath again. But on this occasion, she was not as well as usual. For the first time since I knew her, she had not made her annual trip to America in the autumn. Instead, she had decided to go to Bath just before Christmas, not in February as usual. Then I had a letter from her saying if I was not doing anything special, could I go down to Bath, "to cheer up an old lady". I wrote back to her, saying I could not possibly leave my wife and three children. In reply, a telegram arrived the next day. "Dumb head, I mean wife too, letter following". That second letter suggested I leave my children with a relative, all expenses to be met by her.

This time, my wife and I drove to Bath in my new three hundred pound Vauxhall car. Again, we did not sleep at the same hotel as Mrs Cavalier-Smith. But we had dinner with her every night, just as before. The Duke of Connaught was staying at her hotel that time. So was the daughter of the Emperor of Abyssinia. She nodded to my wife and myself one evening, as we were standing outside on the steps of the hotel.

On Christmas Day there was a big party. A dressed pig's head decorated the table. Everything you could imagine in the way of food and drink was available. Afterwards the tables were cleared away and a conjuror appeared to entertain us. Our seats were on the front row but the conjuror decided he needed a little more room for his act. Very politely, he asked the three of us to move our chairs back. By this time, Mrs Cavalier-Smith had drunk a little too much brandy and whisky. This was a habit she had got into recently. Basically, she was now a very lonely woman. All her relatives were in America. Her friends in this country had either died or were now too infirm to visit. Mrs Cavalier-Smith refused to move her chair back and shouted at him very loudly in a rather rude voice, "Certainly not."

The hotel was not the sort of place where you behaved like that. Totally embarrassed, she rushed out of the room, ran into the ladies' toilet and locked herself in one of the cubicles. There she stayed, absolutely refusing to budge. She was finally rescued by one of the maids. She went into the adjacent cubicle, clambered over the partition and opened the door. But, next day, nobody said a word about it. It was as though everything was all forgotten. Mrs Cavalier-Smith hired a chauffeur-driven car and the three of us spent the rest of the week sightseeing. We went everywhere, including Wells Cathedral and Glastonbury Tor.

After we returned home Mrs Cavalier-Smith's health began to deteriorate. Over the next few months she often sent for me to sit with her of an evening. My wife, too, was often called on to keep her company. Early on in the following summer I had the sad task of writing to her two daughters in America. I had to tell them to come to England right away, as their mother was dying. One of them managed to get to Chivers three days before she passed away. I noticed that shortly before she died Mrs Cavalier-Smith had her silver tea service expertly cleaned, then she passed it on to a long-standing friend.

By this time, I had worked for Mrs Cavalier-Smith for eighteen years. She had made me one of the executors of her will. As an executor, I had the responsibility of helping to make arrangements for her funeral. I went with her daughter to the parish churchyard in Stondon Massey. Together, we chose the place where her mother would be buried. I marked it out with a miniature iron fence.

Mrs Cavalier-Smith was laid to rest on the thirteenth of August in the year 1939. She was seventy-seven. That day would have been her birthday. It was my birthday. It was my wife's birthday. But it wasn't a very happy day for either of us. Immediately after the funeral, I took Mrs Cavalier-Smith's daughter to Brentwood Station. She wanted to get back to America. That evening I met Mrs Cavalier-Smith's other daughter and that daughter's husband at the same station. The two sisters were estranged and never met or spoke to each other. On the way back to Chivers, I had to point out to this daughter that the car she was riding in was mine, as she seemed keen to sell it quickly. It was, most definitely, not part of her mother's estate I told her.

Next day I was cutting flowers in the gardens at Chivers when the daughter's husband walked past. He remarked he had an idea where I intended taking them. I knew there was an old vase in a cupboard in the kitchen. It was worth only a few pence. But, it would hold the flowers I had cut, so I could put them on Mrs Cavalier-Smith's grave. Thinking it only right to get the daughter's permission first before I took the vase, I went indoors and explained why I wanted it. But the daughter refused to let me have it. So I went home, got my wife's celery vase and used that instead. A week later, I asked one of the outdoor staff to cut some turf and put it in my car and I took it along to the churchyard. I was putting it on Mrs Cavalier-Smith's grave when my eldest son came cycling along the road. Mrs Cavalier-Smith's daughter wanted me back at Chivers immediately. I told him to tell her I would come back there when I had finished.

I discovered the reason for the urgency when I returned to Chivers. The outbreak of a second world war seemed to be getting closer and closer by the day. Mrs Cavalier-Smith's daughter and her husband were now desperate to leave England and return to America. A telephone message had just been received. They had managed to obtain reservations on the *Aquitania*. But the ship was due to sail for New York that very evening. Could I drive them to Southampton docks right away?

They seemed to have more faith in my ability to get them there on time, than the chauffeur's. I asked the chauffeur to get one of the cars ready. Then I went home to change. When I got back to Chivers, I found an enormous suitcase had been strapped to the luggage rack at the back of the car. I told one of the gardeners to take the suitcase back indoors. I pointed out to the daughter that, as an executor of her mother's will, I had every right to know what items she was removing from the house. I rang the solicitor handling Mrs Cavalier-Smith's estate. He said I should make a list of the contents of the suitcase and their total value would be debited against the daughter's share of the estate.

As we set off for Southampton, the two of them, the daughter and her husband, promised to provide me with a lunch on the way, as I was rushing away without my midday meal. They never did. When the car was refilled with petrol, I paid. When we stopped at a pub and the three of us had a drink, I paid. On getting to the docks, we discovered the *Aquitania* was not sailing that evening after all. In view of the tense international situation, the boat had to wait until morning so she could be escorted across the Atlantic by a warship.

We found a hotel close by, then the daughter's husband sent me back to the docks. He had forgotten to confirm their reservations and collect their tickets. I had not eaten since early morning and was getting hungrier and hungrier, so I took the opportunity to sneak into a café and gulp down two eggs and bacon. I returned to find the two of them seated in the hotel's dining room, eating an enormous meal. The daughter said she had booked me into the chauffeurs' quarters. I would have to go round to the hotel's back entrance. I told her that her mother would never have done that to me. I also said I was going home immediately. Her husband pulled out his wallet and shook hands with me. While doing so, he slipped me a note. When I looked, I saw it was worth ten shillings. I went back to Essex, rang the solicitor and reclaimed all the money I had spent on the journey. A few days later the Second World War started. All Mrs Cavalier-Smith's property in England was put up for sale. But nobody was interested in buying anything, when the future seemed so uncertain. Chivers and its land, even with the two farms included, fetched very little, nothing like their true value. Eventually, a local farmer bought the lot. I think he paid around two and a half thousand pounds for them. The contents of the house were also sold off. I went to the auction held at Chivers and managed to buy a few small china dishes as keepsakes.

In her will, Mrs Cavalier-Smith left me five hundred pounds and the small semi-detached cottage she had originally built for me: the one in which I had first lived. At the time she signed her will, I was still actually living there. After I moved into Chivers Lodge, the detached house she had built for me later, she told me she had signed a codicil leaving that house to me as well. But I was not present when one of her daughters opened her will. As an executor I should have been. The daughter claimed no codicil had been found. So eventually I had to move out of Chivers Lodge and back into the smaller Chivers Cottage. But I paid a builder to do some alterations to make it bigger. When these were finished I renamed the place Cavalier Cottage, in memory of Mrs Cavalier-Smith. It was the only memorial she had.

CHAPTER
TWENTY

I was forty-six. I had no job. And the country was getting involved in a second world war. This time I was too old to fight. But I was still young enough for the authorities to be interested in me. They expected me to contribute to the country's war effort in some way. So I enlisted as a Special Constable for a short while. Then I became a member of the War Reserve, a sort of home army. We had the task of guarding strategic sites that the enemy might favour as potential worthwhile targets. I had to have a medical examination and be passed as totally fit, before I could be issued with my black uniform, heavy boots and smart peaked cap.

Almost immediately, I experienced my first daylight air raid. I was on duty at North Weald Radio Station, not far from Ongar, the small town where I signed the unemployment register all those years ago. I was standing at the station's main gate, quietly enjoying a cup of tea, kindly offered by the lady living opposite, when without any warning a squadron of German bombers swooped down low out of the clouds. I was scared stiff. Immediately, I jumped into a nearby ditch, crouched down, and pressed my body as close to the bottom of the ditch as it would go.

Bombs began falling like a shower of confetti, all over the place. I felt the ground under me shaking, almost rocking with their impact. A woman came running along the road, dragging a child. It was screaming with fright. I leapt out and pulled both of them into the ditch with me. The German planes circled one more time overhead, then left. Immediately, the telephone at the main gate rang. It was Curly Waller, another member of the War Reserve, asking if I was all right. Curly could get meat from somewhere, so I got steaks when we were on duty together.

But the army took over guard duties at the radio station and I was transferred. I was still in the War Reserve but I was now part of the police force in Ongar. My job was to patrol the streets of the small town. I did not enjoy it one little bit. I hated patrolling. The air raids were becoming more frequent. More and more bombs were being dropped, making more and more terrific loud bangs as they exploded. The noise began to bring back unpleasant memories: the bombardments I had experienced on the front line in the First World War. The gas attack. Dead and injured men lying everywhere, pleading for assistance. The shooting of my two mates.

The patrolling of the town was organised into three shifts. Each lasted eight hours. One was from ten o'clock at night until six o'clock the next morning, another from six o'clock in the morning until two in the afternoon. The third was from two o'clock in the afternoon until ten that evening. One night I was on duty at Marden Ash, an area on the outskirts of Ongar.

It was almost ten o'clock. I was looking forward to someone relieving me in a few minutes at the end of my shift when the sirens sounded, giving advance warning of a German air raid. I did what I was supposed to do when this happened. I made my way to the police station in the centre of the town. Sergeant Smith, the man in charge there, told me to go straight back to Marden Ash and remain at my post until I was officially relieved. My replacement did not arrive until two o'clock in the morning, four hours late. He informed me I would be expected to resume duty again in exactly four hours time, at six in the morning. I returned to the police station and complained to Sergeant Smith. He said I had got to do it. So I knocked at the Superintendent's door and told him. He said nine o'clock would do. But I had made up my mind. I wanted to leave the police force. I went to see Dr. Wilson, a good friend of mine. He lived in Ongar. He examined me and signed a certificate saying I was unfit for duty. I finished with the War Reserve at the end of the week. I could now enjoy peaceful days at home. I had enough to live on. I had my savings and what Mrs Cavalier-Smith had left me.

Everyone was being encouraged to grow more food. I was happy to pass the time looking after vegetables in my garden. But the authorities caught up with me again. I had another letter. I was still required to make my contribution to the war effort. Ambulance driving or rescue work were the two things offered me.

After a test drive, I was taken on as an ambulance driver, a job I did for the rest of the war. I had to go into Brentwood every Tuesday night and sleep in a bunk bed in a council hut. I remember one night being called out from there because there was an air raid on the town and a house had been hit by a bomb. A member of the rescue squad, Mr Everett, whom I knew, was waiting for me when I got there. He indicated there was a fatality. The body was brought out and put beside the ambulance. It seemed to be that of a grey-haired man of about sixty. As an ambulance driver, I was not allowed touch it. Only the rescue squad could do that. Mr Everett went back inside the house and came out with a pair of slippers. He put them on the dead man's feet, telling him he would feel a lot better now. Looking back now, it seems funny he should have done it. But it was a wartime situation and people seem to react differently when faced with sudden death.

As chairman of the ex-servicemen's club, I was helping to organise entertainment for the soldiers stationed in the area. All nationalities were represented, but Americans troops far outnumbered all the others. Dances were held regularly at the ex-service men's club. The music came from popular gramophone records. The Americans, in particular, loved "jitterbugging" to them with the local girls.

A few of us used to meet and arrange special fund raising dances and whist drives at the ex-service men's hall. We did this throughout the war. The money we raised we sent to the young men and women from Stondon Massey who were away serving in the forces. We used to send them a five-shilling postal order every few weeks. It was not much but it helped. The pay for ordinary ranks in the armed forces was not generous, so they were very pleased to get it. But we had to work very hard to keep the money coming in, so we could do it.

After the war ended we continued to raise money for a hardship fund. If you raised a certain amount, the Government contributed a further portion. The fund gave financial help to any ex-members of the forces and their families living in the village, if they were having problems settling back into normal civilian life again. Perhaps they could not get work right away. Or through illness or injury could not do the work they did before the war. As a member of the investigating committee, I went round interviewing claimants. Several needed help badly.

Towards the end of the war, I had been offered a job in insurance, which I took. There were not many men left around to do it and I was beginning to realise I might not be as well off as I thought. There were not many things I could do. I was a gardener. Always had been. Always would be. Gardening was what I had been trained to do. Gardening was what I had spent my working life doing. But I knew by the time the war was over, I would probably not get another gardening job. I would be too old and I had begun to suspect there would hardly be any of my sort of jobs around. Even fewer than after the First World War. Not at Head Gardener level. Not at any level. There did not seem to be any private country estates left any more. The employment ladder they provided had gone along with them.

I worked at my insurance job for a good number of years. At the same time, I was continuing to act as Chairman of the Trustees of the Stondon Massey and District Ex-servicemen's Club and Chairman of the organising committee. I held both posts for more than twenty years. After the war, I got further involved in local community affairs. I became a member of Stondon Massey Parish Council. I found local people constantly sought my advice and were grateful if someone took a friendly interest in their affairs when they needed help. As a long-standing resident of the area, my local knowledge often proved valuable when problems arose. I was also invited to become a manager of the village school in Kelvedon Hatch. The school was attended by the children of Stondon Massey as well, because that village no longer had a school of its own.

My mother died in 1956. She was eighty-six and had been a widow for thirty-five years. She left a letter addressed to us four children. Her writing shows she must have been very weak when she wrote it. It also shows that the second part was not written at the same time as the first. It reads, "My dear children, I do wish to thank you all so much for the love and care that you have bestowed upon me since your father died. I cannot thank you enough for all that you have done for me. I do hope you will all try and keep together as you have always done. With dear love to all, from a grateful mother."

I was a member of Stondon Massey Parish Council for twenty-four years, being chairman for some of them. A special presentation was made to me on my retirement from the Board of Managers of Kelvedon Hatch school, after having served twenty-five years.

When I was eighty-four, I felt an urge to go back to Amoneburg, in Germany. I wanted to see how much, if at all, the village had changed in the intervening sixty or so years. I wondered whether the baker's shop, where I had worked as a prisoner of war, was still there. I wanted to discover, if possible, what had happened to the people I had known. My daughter Sheila drove me there. We found the baker's shop. It was still almost the same as I remembered it. The oven had been modernised. No-one need any longer spend the morning splitting wood with a wedge and a mallet to feed the fire that baked the bread and cakes.

The new owner, a relative of Herr Weitzel, invited me into the back room, the one where I used to eat my evening meal of potatoes and sour milk with Herr Weitzel and Frau Kleam, both now long dead. Gretchen's father's guesthouse, Gasthaus Greib, still flourished over the road. It had survived the Second World War almost intact, having been machine gunned once by a passing allied plane. No rooms were available there for the first night of my stay, but I was able to move in for a night or two later. I was told Herr von Creipe, Gretchen's father, too, was dead. I asked for news of Gretchen herself. She had married, a few years after I left, and moved away to a city. But she died suddenly when she was just twenty-eight. The woman now running the guesthouse had been Gretchen's sister-in-law. She was now married to her second husband.

176

Amoneburg itself seemed to have changed very little. But there were no cows pulling farm implements along the roads. Just small mechanised tractors running smoothly along streets, whose cobblestones had all been covered in tarmac. The church I had attended regularly while a prisoner of war was still there. I went to one of the services on the Sunday. The women, working in the small local fields, were another familiar sight.

Back home again, I continued to live with Ethel, my wife, at Cavalier Cottage. I pass the time tending my garden and exchanging visits with younger members of my family. I drove my car until I was ninety-three. I still put flowers on Mrs Cavalier-Smith's grave on her birthday, as I have done every year since her death

When my wife and I celebrated our seventieth wedding anniversary, Kelvedon Hatch Parochial Church Council gave a lunch party for us. Both of us had attended church regularly throughout our married lives, but services had not been held on a regular basis in Stondon Massey church, our local one, for some years, so we started to go to the one in Kelvedon Hatch.

Today, if anyone asks me about my life, I always give the same reply. I think it has been a very full and very happy one. In many ways, I think I was very fortunate to have been born the son of a Bailiff on a private country estate.

POSTSCRIPT

Finally, Jack was taken ill and admitted to hospital. Members of his family stayed with him, in turn, throughout his short stay. He died there in the arms of one of his sons, the day being the eighteenth of April and the year 1993. He was just four months short of his hundredth birthday. But, as his daughter said, he had seen a hundred Christmases. His wife, his children, grandchildren and other members of his family, along with his friends, filled St Nicholas Church in Kelvedon Hatch for the funeral service and later watched his interment in the churchyard.

As memories of the war receded and the number of ex-servicemen in the area declined, the future of the club Jack helped to establish had to be considered. Events the committee held at their small meeting place no longer attracted the local following they once had. Television had begun offering people entertainment at home. More were beginning to have their own personal transport and could sample entertainment further afield if they wished. As Chairman of the Trustees, Jack had what was to him the sad task of helping to negotiate the hall's takeover by Brentwood District

Council. In time, the simple wooden structure, the original home of the Stondon Massey and District ex-service men's club, was demolished. The modern brick building erected in its place is now known as Tipps Cross Remembrance Hall. It is available for hire by local community groups and a club for local teenagers is based there.

No trace of Mushroom Hall remains. That, too, has been demolished. This happened before the days when a preservation order might have been obtained to ensure its survival.

Porters Park, where Mr Raphael used to host his regular dinner parties and his annual servants ball and cultivate his carnations, was sold to Middlesex County Council in 1926. From then on it was known as Shenley Mental Hospital.

Warren House, where Baroness Bischoffsheim once entertained the country's top political and military leaders and cultivated her orchids, is now an Islamic Centre.

Hatch Farm, the lovely big old house where Jack's wife lived with her aunt as a child, has been turned into offices.

The Perpetual Flowering Carnation Society, of which Mr Cecil Raphael was a Vice President, has been renamed and is now known as the British National Carnation Society.

The church at All Saints Convent begun by the architect Sir Ninian Comper in 1922 was not completed until 1962 by his son. But only eight years after its consecration, the nuns left the Convent. They moved to a much smaller home in Birmingham. By that time, their numbers had declined and so few Sisters were living at the Convent, it was no longer feasible for them to remain there any longer.

But the nuns wanted the convent and its remaining seventy acres, which included their burial ground, to stay in religious hands, so they passed them to the Roman Catholic Church. They accepted three hundred thousand pounds, half their estimated full commercial value at that time, to ensure this happened. So the remains of the little chapel on Chantry Island returned to the church under which it was originally founded. Today the Convent is a retreat and pastoral centre, open to groups or individuals of all denominations who wish to spend a few quiet days there. A member of staff lives in Jack's old home, now remodelled inside

Both Chivers, separated from its two farms, and Chivers Lodge, now no longer connected in any way to the former "big house", remain family homes.

Jack's widow and daughter continued to live at Cavalier Cottage until the death of Jack's widow.

The gardening tradition in Jack's family has been maintained by his oldest son. He cultivates his very large garden in his leisure time, selling his produce from his home. One of Jack's grandsons has studied horticulture at college and is now a member of the gardening staff of a local council.

Also available in ISIS Large Print:

A Romany in the Fields

G. Bramwell Evens

Preferring to "loiter in green meadows" discussing the balance of nature with John the Gamekeeper and learning tricks from Jerry the Poacher, Romany dons his brown tweed suit and sets off on a journey through the seasons of the countryside.

Along the way, we learn about the bravery of mother hares and how moles store worms, and watch lambs have their first taste of milk. We also see how the countryside changes from one season to another, from crisp snow to the rich colours of autumn.

ISBN 0-7531-9316-7 (hb)
ISBN 0-7531-9317-5 (pb)

The Green Years

Mollie Harris

One of seven children, Mollie Harris was brought up in the Oxfordshire village of Ducklington. She tells of the joys and hardships of life in her poor, hard-working family, from stealing plums from the neighbour's garden, to being given the "swillings" of a jam jar as a treat.

Full of captivating tales of hot days by the river and cold winters in the classroom, of friends and family and of life in the village, this is an unforgettable account of a country childhood.

ISBN 0-7531-9346-9 (hb)
ISBN 0-7531-9347-7 (pb)

A Midhurst Lad

Ronald E. Boxall

Although poverty and illness marred his young life, the author's sense of mischief and humour shine through this charming childhood autobiography.

Born into the Boxall family in 1924, Ronald was brought up in Duck Lane, Midhurst at that time an address synonymous with hardship. The tale of "the average life of an average boy born of poor parents, who lived under slum conditions, yet dwelt in the centre of a tiny and pretty town set in a near paradise of pastoral and sylvan delights", Ronald tells his story with natural wit and clarity, sharing his memories of a bygone age.

ISBN 0-7531-9320-5 (hb)
ISBN 0-7531-9321-3 (pb)

A Romany on the Trail

G. Bramwell Evens

Romany is back on the trail in another collection of tales from the countryside. He draws us into fellowship with the fur and feather folk of hedgerow and heath, field and river-bank, wood and moor, and he shows us hidden wonder and hidden meaning.

From glorious pine forests with carpets of needles, to early lambs and night fishing, we share all of Romany and Raq's experiences. We also meet their friends, Jerry the Poacher, Sally Stordy, Ned the village postman and many others.

ISBN 0-7531-9314-0 (hb)
ISBN 0-7531-9315-9 (pb)